ROSE ELLIOT'S

MOTHER, BABY & TODDLER BOOK

ROSE ELLIOT'S

MOTHER, BABY & TODDLER BOOK

A UNIQUE GUIDE TO RAISING A BABY ON A HEALTHY VEGETARIAN DIET

Some of the material included in this book has been previously
published in the UK as
ROSE ELLIOT'S MOTHER AND BABY BOOK (Thorsons 1993)
and subsequently as
ROSE ELLIOT'S MOTHER, BABY AND TODDLER BOOK
(HarperCollins 1996).

This fully revised and updated version is published in 2003 by
Hochland Communications Ltd.

Front Cover photograph provided by: Powerstock
Back Cover photograph provided by:
THISLIFE PICTURES/Angela Maynard
Other photographs provided by:
THISLIFE PICTURES/Angela Maynard
Food Features

Design by: Gwilym Hughes

ISBN 1-904038-09-3

Printed in Spain by: Bookprint S.L.

CONTENTS

Author's Note

Like all writers of books about babies, I had to face the problem of what pronoun to use when referring to the baby. Determined not to be sexist, I started by calling the baby 'it'. But that didn't sound right, so in line with a number of recent babycare books - and since I myself have three daughters - I eventually settled on 'she'.

To mothers of baby sons, I apologise if this seems inappropriate, and hope you'll mentally read 'he' instead.

Acknowledgements

I'd like to express my love and gratitude to my mother, Joan Hodgson, whose mothering was the pattern and model for my own; and to my husband and three daughters, without whom this book certainly wouldn't have been written. My grateful thanks, too, to all the people who have encouraged and helped me in writing this book in its various forms over the years: the Vegetarian Society (UK) for getting me started and also for their help and support with this edition, especially Niki O'Leary and Chris Olivant for their useful comments and help with this edition; Fontana (and especially Helen Fraser) for publishing the original UK edition of Rose Elliot's Vegetarian Mother and Baby Book; Vivienne Schuster, my agent at that time; Dr Alan Long for advice on nutrition; Juliet Gellately for information on soya milk; Wendy Wolf and Juliet Annan of Pantheon for making the first US edition possible and for all their ideas and suggestions; to Polly Powell, Barbara Dixon and Kelly Davis for ideas and help. Most especially I'd like to thank Henry Hochland for making this new edition possible, Heather Stackhouse for all her careful editing, ideas, hard work and tremendous enthusiasm which have contributed so much to this edition; also to Gwilym Hughes who has done such a fantastic job on the design and Angela Maynard for her exquisite mother-and-baby photographs; to Food Features for the food photographs and to Powerstock for the beautiful cover picture; my agent, Barbara Levy, and Gill Thorn, my birth counsellor when I had Claire, and dear friend ever since, for reading through both the original and the current manuscript and making many valuable suggestions.

PART 1

NUTRITION AND BABYCARE

INTRODUCTION

You're vegetarian (or vegan) and you're pregnant or planning to have a baby soon; or maybe you've already had your baby. You want to know how your diet will affect your baby and how to bring him or her up to be really healthy.

The good news is that you're not alone. Many of us have done it and lively fifth-generation vegetarian and vegan babies are now being born. But of course you want to know the best foods to choose and how to go about getting your baby from milk to solid food – and that's what this book is all about, crammed with all the tips I've gleaned from my own experience of having three babies, and now five grandchildren – all of them vegetarian, clever, healthy and energetic, as I'm sure yours will be.

In this book I'm first of all going to give an over-view of the foods which make up a vegetarian diet and show how you can get all the essential nutrients. We'll see what this means in terms of a day's eating then look at how you need to vary the basic diet in preparation for conception, during pregnancy and when breast-feeding. After that we'll follow the progress of your baby from birth to two years; and in the second part of the book you'll find the recipes to put it all into practice.

the essential
nutrients

...what they are and where to find them

In this section we're going to look at the nutrients we need to be strong and healthy, and where we can get them in a vegetarian or vegan diet. First of all, though, let's just consider what nutrients we, as vegetarians or vegans, might be missing. By not eating meat and fish we're cutting out two major sources of protein. In addition, meat supplies fat, some B vitamins and some minerals - mainly iron, potassium, phosphorus and zinc and fish provides vitamins A, D, E, some essential omega oils and the mineral iodine. If we don't eat dairy produce either, we also need to look carefully at alternative sources of calcium, riboflavin, vitamin D and B12. It's perfectly possible to get all these nutrients from a vegetarian or vegan diet. Here's how:

■ PROTEIN

Protein is essential for growth and repair of body cells; for reproduction, making blood and bones and for protection against infection. Women need 45-60g of protein a day, men need 55-65g. Best vegetarian sources are:
— *NUTS:* almonds, brazils, cashews, walnuts, pinenuts, hazelnuts, peanuts, including butters made from them such as almond butter, peanut butter etc
— *SEEDS:* sesame seeds and tahini, or sesame paste; pumpkin seeds and pumpkin butter, sunflower seeds, linseeds
— *PULSES:* lentils, peas and beans (technically peanuts belong here, but I've put them with the nuts as they behave more like a nut, and that's how we think of them)
— *SOYA:* yes, soya is a pulse, but I've listed it separately because it's particularly high in protein and because it can be found in so many forms: tofu, tempeh, textured vegetable protein, soya milk, soya yoghurt
— *MYCOPROTEINS:* such as Quorn. Check on the packet to make sure they are approved by the Vegetarian Society as some have battery-egg white added
— *DAIRY PRODUCTS:* milk, cheese, yoghurt
— *EGGS*

Protein is made up of about 20 units called amino acids. Our bodies can make most of these but there are eight that it can't make: these are called essential amino acids. As long as we eat these in some form or other our body can mix and match to make the perfect protein for its needs. It takes proteins from all kinds of foods - the ones listed above, potatoes, vegetables, fruit and most particularly from grains and cereals. Grains and cereals consist mainly of carbohydrate with just a little protein. However the protein they do have contains the essential amino acids which are missing from pulses, so they are particularly valuable.

You really don't have to worry about this mixing and matching of protein, though. It happens almost automatically because in fact we mix proteins all the time. It happens naturally in dishes like beans on toast, hummus and pitta bread, pasta and lentils, muesli and milk, spicy rice and dal - I could go on. And even if you don't manage to get all the essential amino acids at one meal, it doesn't matter because it's now been discovered that the body has a temporary store from which it can draw. To make sure you get enough protein, have a varied diet and aim to include a good source of protein at every meal.

■ CARBOHYDRATE

All carbohydrate consists of sugars, which our body extracts and uses for energy. Refined carbohydrate foods such as white sugar, fizzy drinks, sweets, white flour products like bread, cakes and biscuits are quickly digested so the sugar goes straight into our blood stream. We get an almost immediate energy-boost followed by a dip not long afterwards, when we want more carbohydrate to lift us up again.

Complex carbohydrate foods such as wholemeal bread and pasta, brown rice, oats, millet, barley, buckwheat, quinoa (a valuable grain), and all the pulses (lentil, beans etc which are half protein, half carbohydrate) is also broken down into sugars. The big difference is that with these complex carbohydrates it happens slowly. The natural bran and fibre in them means that it takes longer for the body to extract the sugars and they get into our blood stream in smaller amounts over a longer period of time.

12

This slow absorption is the healthy way. If sugar gets into the bloodstream too quickly the body has to take emergency action, releasing a great deal of insulin to deal with the sugar. While this may be all right occasionally, there is growing evidence to suggest that repeatedly straining the body in this way can upset the delicate mechanism that controls the flow of insulin, resulting in diabetes.

The fibre, which prevents unrefined carbohydrates from being digested too quickly, also absorbs water like a sponge and provides bulk as it travels along the digestive tract. This means the muscles of the intestine can get a good grip, move it along smoothly, quickly, and efficiently so we don't get constipated.

■ FATS AND OILS
We need fat for the absorption of some vitamins, to make some hormones and to keep our tissues healthy. Like proteins, fats are made up of smaller units called fatty acids and two of these are known as essential fatty acids. These are linoleic acid (omega 6) and linolenic acid (omega 3).

We need both these oils in our body and they're both healthy. The trouble is most of us have too much omega 6 and not enough omega 3. This is because omega 6 is present in the vegetable oils which are used in the manufacture of food – ovenchips, ready-meal, cakes and biscuits – and there are very few sources of omega 3.

Even if you don't eat the foods I've mentioned, you're unlikely to have a problem getting enough linoleic acid, (omega 6) as it's in most nuts, seeds and plant foods. Linolenic, omega 3, is the one which non-vegetarians can get from oily fish and which vegetarians can get from flax or linseeds and their oil, walnuts and walnut oil, cold-pressed rapeseed oil. They must be unheated to get the benefit. These contain 'short-chain' omega 3 oils, which our body can convert to the long-chain omega 3 oils which it needs. Long-chain omega 3 oils are found in some blue-green algae and you can buy this in supplement form either as capsules or as a dry 'superfood'. I advise any

vegetarian or vegan to consider taking these in addition to the 'short-chain' omega 3 oils which not everyone can convert efficiently to 'long chain' fatty acids. I believe they are especially important to take during pregnancy and breast -feeding, for the healthy development of the baby's brain.

So I advise:
– a heaped tablespoonful of finely ground flax seeds every day or you could do what I do and take either cold-pressed flax seed oil or one of the omega oil blends like Udo's oils.
– a daily dose of a supplement containing long-chain omega 3 oils.

If you think you may be a bit lacking in omega 3's, start with the flax seed oil, then after 2-3 months go on to the balanced oil. I take 2 tablespoons every day. You can pour it over things or mix it into a salad dressing but I find the flavour too strong and prefer just to take it from a spoon followed by a drink of water. Be sure that the oil you get is really fresh and always keep it in the fridge: these nutritious oils go off very quickly.

– the healthiest oil to use on salad dressings and shallow-frying is extra virgin olive oil

– for deep-frying, groundnut or rapeseed (canola in the US) oil, which are the most stable at high temperatures. Ghee or clarified butter are also stable when heated. Coconut oil has many health properties and is said to be excellent for cooking at high temperatures but I haven't had a chance to experiment with it yet

The reason for my choice of fats is that when vegetable oils are heated, as happens during the refining process and in the making of margarine, the chemical structure of the molecules is altered, producing trans-fatty acids, which are harmful to health. There appears to be a link between high intake of trans-fatty acids and some cancers. Fats such as butter, olive oil, groundnut and rapeseed oil, on the other hand, are chemically more stable when heated, so I prefer to use them for cooking.

13

■ VITAMINS

Vitamins are substances that are essential for good health. The body cannot make them, or only in small quantities; a deficiency in any of them can result in a number of minor ailments and impaired health and growth, especially in children.

Vitamin A (or Beta Carotene)

Necessary for healthy eyes, skin, lungs, throat, hair and nails; increases resistance to disease and helps healing. Found in:
- red, orange and yellow vegetables and fruit like peppers and carrots, sweet potato, apricots, peaches, oranges and in leafy green vegetables
- dairy produce, egg yolk and fortified margarine

B Vitamins

Are essential for healthy blood, muscles, nerves, eyes, hair, skin, brain and adrenal glands, also for digestion and metabolism. They include B1 (thiamine), B2 (riboflavin), B3 (niacin), B6 (pyridoxine), B12 (cycanocobalamin), folate, pantothenic acid and biotin. With the exception of B12 they tend to occur together in the same foods and are found in:
- yeast, whole cereals and grains, especially wheatgerm
- nuts and seeds
- pulses
- green vegetables

Some studies have shown that vegans can be short of riboflavin, so if you don't eat dairy, make a special effort to eat the foods mentioned above. Mushrooms, almonds, yeast and yeast extracts, buckwheat, wheatgerm, quinoa, millet and spinach are particularly rich sources.

B12 is found in eggs and dairy produce, and in many foods which are fortified with this vitamin: most yeast extracts, some breakfast cereals, veggieburgers and some soya milks (read the labels). If you're vegan, or a vegetarian who isn't eating much dairy produce you need to include these foods or to take a supplement which is easily obtainable.

Vitamin C

Important for resistance to infection and is needed for the absorption of iron, tissue repair and normal growth. Vitamin C is found in:
- fresh fruit and vegetables, especially citrus fruit and juice, cantaloupe melon, kale, kiwi fruit, red peppers, strawberries, tomatoes, cabbage and broccoli. A 125ml/4fl oz serving of orange juice supplies daily needs (although a lot of nutritionists would argue that you can go a lot higher than this with beneficial results).

Vitamin C is easily lost through exposure to air, heat and water but even cooked cabbage (and also potato) supplies useful amounts. A normal vegetarian or vegan diet, with its abundance of fruits and vegetables, is unlikely to be lacking in this vitamin.

Vitamin D

Needed in order to use calcium efficiently for teeth and bones. We can get this vitamin both from foods and from the action of sunlight on our skin:
- naturally present in eggs, butter, milk, cheese, yoghurt and cottage cheese; while margarine and some breakfast cereals are fortified with it

Some experts believe that you can get sufficient from food and from the action of sunlight on the skin but, unless you live in a very sunny part of the world, it's best not to rely on this source. People with dark skins cannot absorb vitamin D from sunshine, so they can become deficient in vitamin D.

Many experts recommend a daily vitamin D supplement for everyone, whether vegetarian or not, and I think this is sensible advice, especially for young children and old people. But if you are taking any general vitamin tablets, check whether these contain vitamin D before adding any extra to your normal healthy vegetarian diet; and if you're taking a vitamin D supplement do seek advice, because excessive vitamin D is toxic.

Vitamin E

Improves general vitality and is important for the functioning of the heart. It may help to avoid atherosclerosis (hardening of the arteries) and high blood pressure. It is also said to increase fertility, help prevent varicose veins, and improve the body's ability to heal itself.
— best sources of vitamin E are wheatgerm, wholegrain cereals, nuts and seeds

Vitamin K

Necessary for blood clotting and is found in:
— leafy green vegetables, cereals, tomatoes, soya oil, egg yolks. Our body also makes it in the intestine. A daily serving of leafy green vegetables will make sure that you have an adequate amount of this vitamin

■ MINERALS

There are 15 minerals which are essential for the health of the body. Some of the most important are:

Iron

Needed for the formation of blood and for carrying oxygen in the blood; lack of iron can cause anaemia. Iron deficiency in women is one of the most common problems in the British diet but scientific studies have shown that vegetarians and vegans are no more likely to suffer from this than meat eaters.
In a vegetarian diet, iron is obtained from:
— pulses (soya beans and lentils are excellent sources); soya flour
  wholegrain cereals, especially wholemeal bread and millet (which is the most iron-rich grain)
— nuts and seeds
— dark green vegetables
— dried fruits (apricots, peaches and prunes are particularly good sources)
— Brewers' yeast, molasses and wheatgerm are concentrated sources
A vegetarian or vegan diet planned along the lines suggested on p18 will meet the recommended iron levels. Although vegetable sources of iron are less well absorbed than animal sources, taking them with a rich source of vitamin C, such as orange juice, helps.

Calcium

Needed for the health of bones, skin and teeth and for the functioning of the heart. It is also involved in blood clotting. The richest sources of calcium are:
— milk, cheese and yoghurt
— tap water in hard water areas and some bottled waters, e.g. Evian (read the labels)
— nuts and seeds, especially sesame seeds and of course sesame cream (tahini) and hummus made with plenty of tahini
— leafy green vegetables, especially kale and purple sprouting broccoli
— dried fruit, especially figs

It's not difficult for vegetarians to obtain enough from these sources but if you're a vegan, make sure you're using a calcium-enriched soya milk and yoghurt and eat some calcium-rich green leafy vegetables and a few dried figs or sesame seeds every day. These foods, together with the grains, wholemeal bread, nuts, fruits, pulses and vegetables that make up a day's healthy eating, should ensure that your needs are met. The evidence is that, although vegans consume less calcium in their food, their bodies use it and store it more efficiently than those of meat eaters.

Zinc

Vitally important for normal growth, healing and the immune system. A deficiency often manifests as white flecks on the fingernails and skin problems, such as eczema and acne. Make a point of including in your diet foods that are rich in this mineral. The best sources are:
— cheese
— sesame and pumpkin seeds
— lentils
— wholegrain cereals and wheatgerm

Studies show that vegetarians and vegans consume as much if not more zinc than meat eaters do.

Iodine

Essential for the proper functioning of the thyroid gland. Found in:

- dairy products: about half the iodine consumption in the UK comes from these
- seaweeds and foods made from them such as Vecon, a vegetable stock concentrate/spread like a yeast extract, vegetarian jelling agents, such as agar
- iodised table salt

In Canada all table salt is iodised and in the US iodised table salt is widely available and some products are fortified with iodine. However in the UK there is no policy for iodine fortification and vegan diets can be too low in iodine unless supplements, iodine-rich seaweeds or foods containing these (like Vecon,) are consumed. Don't go overboard though because too much iodine is as bad as too little. If you're using seaweed as a regular source of iodine, you don't need an iodised salt as well.

The Vegan Society recommends that in the absence of other supplementation you frequently crumble small amounts of seaweed into foods as you're cooking. Seaweeds which have a fairly consistent level of iodine such as kelp (kombu) or hijiki are best and 100g of dried hijiki or 15g of dried kombu provides a year's supply for one person. Don't go over this level, although nori - that flat black seaweed wrapped around sushi - is low in iodine and you can eat several sheets a day without any worries about excess iodine.

■ TO SUM UP

A well-balanced vegetarian or vegan diet can provide all the nutrients we need. Make sure yours is healthy and balanced by having:

- a good serving of protein at every meal
- unrefined grains and cereals e.g. wholemeal bread
- some nuts and seeds every day
- some form of omega 3 oils daily and an omega 3 supplement
- at least one good serving of green vegetables every day

In the next section we will see how it all works out in terms of meals.

Creating a
balanced diet

Here's how vegetarian and vegan nutrients work out over a day, as advocated by the Vegetarian Society. You don't have to keep to this plan rigidly; as long as your diet generally follows these guidelines, you'll have a balanced and healthy diet.

In the following plan, a 'portion' is, for example, a slice of bread, an apple, a glass of milk or two tablespoons of cooked beans or grains. A typical serving at a meal might well consist of more than one portion.

Fruits and Vegetables
5 or more portions daily
Fresh, frozen, juiced, canned or dried fruit and vegetables. Supply, in particular, vitamins, minerals and fibre

Alternatives to Meat and Fish
2-3 portions daily
Include a wide variety of pulses, nuts, seeds, eggs and soya, mycoprotein and wheat proteins in the diet to ensure adequate intakes of protein, minerals and vitamins

Milk and Products
2-3 portions daily
Can be cow's milk and products, or soya milk and yoghurt if you're vegan

Bread, Cereals, Potatoes
5 portions daily
Try to use the wholegrain versions as often as possible and try some of the more unusual and nutritious grains such as millet, buckwheat and quinoa

Essential Fat
1 heaped tablespoonful of finely ground linseeds or 1-2 tablespoons balanced oil every day, plus walnuts and walnut oil

Foods containing sugar
Eat sparingly: the fewer the better

If you build your meals around the foods mentioned, eating a variety of foods, including fruit and vegetables, grains, pulses, nuts and/or seeds, a little fat, with or without dairy produce, you will be healthy and you will get all the nutrients you need.

There are lots of ways you can eat your essential nutrients during the day;
here are some example meals:

BREAKFASTS

— Fresh fruit compote, with a scattering of nuts; wholemeal toast
— Dried and fresh fruit compote with yoghurt or soya yoghurt; wholemeal toast
— Fresh fruit; yoghurt or soya yoghurt; wholemeal toast
— Porridge; fruit juice; wholemeal toast
— Muesli, fruit juice; wholemeal toast
— Scrambled eggs or Scrambled Tofu on toast
— Tofu Potato Cakes or fried smoked tofu with fried tomatoes and mushrooms

LUNCHES

— Greek salad, pitta bread, watercress; apple
— Spinach lasagne, mixed Italian salad; fresh fruit salad
— Hummus and crudités; pitta bread; grapes
— Rice salad with toasted seeds; green salad; pear
— Lentil soup, watercress and yeast extract sandwiches; fresh fruit
— Bean salad with fresh herbs; green salad; fresh berries
— Felafel in pitta pockets with salad and tahini sauce; orange

EVENING MEALS

— Quick chilli with brown rice; green salad; fresh fruit salad with yoghurt or soya yoghurt
— Roasted Mediterranean vegetables, cooked grain, hummus; baked peaches with almonds
— Spaghetti with tomato sauce and Parmesan-style cheese; green salad; apricot fool
— Tofu and peanut satay; lychees and kiwi fruit
— Borlotti beans in coconut milk; brown rice; fresh fruit with apricot sauce
— Barley and mushroom risotto; green salad; rhubarb crumble with custard or yoghurt
— Quinoa pilaff with sundried tomatoes, raisins and pinenuts, mango fool

You will find recipes for all the dishes mentioned above in the recipe section of this book, starting on page 70.

19

Diet for pre-conception, pregnancy and breast-feeding

■ PRECONCEPTION

We all know you can't always control these things, but if you want to have a baby in the near future, it's a very good idea to start preparing for it a few months in advance. Building up your own health and vitality will ensure the best possible start for your baby.

A balanced vegetarian or vegan diet will supply you with the basic nutrients you need for health and vitality. Follow the guidelines given in the previous sections and in addition:

— If you're taking the pill it is strongly recommended that you change to another form of contraception because the pill is known to affect the body's ability to absorb vitamins B6, B2, B12 and folic acid, as well as zinc, copper and iron
— Make sure your intake of vitamins B12 and D is adequate (see p14)
See that you are getting plenty of the other B vitamins, especially folic acid, as well as vitamin E and iron by eating plenty of vegetables, especially leafy green ones, and wholegrain cereals
— If you can get organic produce at this time - perhaps through a 'box' scheme, in which an organic supplier will deliver you a weekly box of assorted seasonal vegetables for a very reasonable price, then so much the better, but even if you can't, still eat lots of fresh fruit and vegetables - all fruit and vegetables are good
— Make sure you're having a good source of protein at every meal
— Now is the time to stop smoking and recreational drugs and to cut back on your consumption of alcohol and caffeine, but drink plenty of water every day

Having done your best, relax, trust yourself and your body and be happy!

■ DIET FOR PREGNANCY

If you've got into the way of eating a really healthy diet before getting pregnant, you'll be off to a really good start and eating well will come naturally to you. Even if you haven't, it's never too late to start, and a wonderful opportunity to improve your diet as you nurture yourself and the new life within you.

During pregnancy, your need for nutrients increases. In particular, you need more iron for the growing baby and to enable your body to make more blood; more calcium and vitamin D; more folate; more protein and, in the last 6 months, more calories. Here's how:

Iron
Make sure you include in your diet plenty of iron-rich foods shown on page 15. If you need a real iron-boost, I love the ideas which Peter Cox suggests for 'intensive iron-snacking' in his Encyclopaedia of Vegetarian Living. These all supply generous amounts of iron:

— Measure 100g/4oz each of dried figs, apricots, dates and prunes into a mixing bowl and cover with water in which 1 tablespoonful of blackstrap molasses has been dissolved. Leave to stand overnight then serve for breakfast, or in small portions throughout the day, with its juice and topped with 1 tablespoonful of pistachios

— Juice 1kg/2lbs organic carrots with 225g/8oz parsley, stalks and all. This is a strong flavour so you may wish to juice this amount in two or three batches during the day. Also, you might try blending it with soya milk and a little apple juice to make it more sweet

— An iron-rich granola can be made by mixing 25g/1oz each of sesame seeds and sunflower seeds and 50g/2oz each of pistachios, pumpkin seeds and rolled oats. Stir in 1 tablespoonful of blackstrap molasses and enough fruit juice to cover and leave to soak. Serve with fresh fruit to taste and eat for

21

breakfast or in small portions throughout the day

— Sauté 450g/1lb of fresh spinach or kale in with some onion and garlic then serve over brown rice. It's not difficult to eat this amount of greens

Calcium and Vitamin D

You need more calcium to build healthy bones and in preparation for breast-feeding. Eat plenty of the calcium-rich foods shown on p.15.

— A simple way of boosting your calcium is to take an extra 350ml/12fl oz milk or calcium-fortified soya milk or the equivalent in yoghurt each day, but if you only eat a little dairy produce or are vegan you might consider taking a calcium supplement, especially if you intend to breast-feed

Normally the action of sunlight on the skin along with dairy products and margarine produces enough vitamin D. However, increased amounts are often recommended for pregnant women and breast-feeding mothers since it works with calcium to form the baby's bones and for milk production. Follow your doctor's advice, as too much vitamin D is toxic.

Folate

Folic acid is essential for the baby's development, and supplements are recommended for all pregnant women during the first three months. Boost your intake by eating:

— leafy green vegetables, lightly cooked or in salads
— wholegrain cereals such as wholemeal bread
— yeast extract, perhaps on wholemeal toast, or use to make wholemeal watercress or cress sandwiches
— dates and nuts
— carrot and parsley juice, if you have a juicer

Protein

Make sure you have a good source of protein at every meal, as explained on p.12. Apart from this,

if you increase your intake of vitamins and minerals as described above, and of calories, as suggested below, you will automatically be getting more protein - even eating the odd extra slice of wholemeal bread adds protein to your diet.

Calories

Funny to be concerned about getting enough calories when it's usually the opposite for many of us! You need about an extra 300kcalories a day in the last six months of pregnancy and if you're enriching your diet in the ways suggested it will probably happen naturally. You may feel extra hungry and need snacks between meals. Some nutritious ideas for snacks are:

— wholemeal watercress sandwiches with yeast extract
— a bowl or mug of lentil soup
— a handful of nuts with dates or other dried fruit
— a piece of fruit bread or a flapjack (p.112)
— some soya or dairy yoghurt with a chopped banana and a sprinkling of chopped almonds or wheatgerm
— a bowl of muesli with milk or soya milk
— wholemeal nut butter sandwiches

Fluid

Finally, make sure you drink enough fluids while you're pregnant; your system is working over-time and needs more. Fresh fruit and vegetable juices, perhaps diluted with water, are good, as are herb teas, cow's milk or soya milk and most of all, lots of water. Its best to restrict or avoid drinks containing caffeine (tea, coffee) and alcohol.

■ TO AVOID DURING PREGNANCY

The Department of Health advises that pregnant women avoid certain foods during pregnancy. These include:
— all unpasteurised milk (cow, sheep or goat)
— soft-whip ice cream
— raw egg (in desserts or home-made mayonnaise)
— vegetable pâté (unless cooked or pasteurised)

- other prepared salads that could be contaminated before purchase
- ripened soft cheeses such as Camembert, Brie and blue-veined varieties

The reason is that all these foods risk contamination from salmonella, listeria or other bacteria. Salmonella leads to food poisoning and in very rare cases listeria can lead to an illness, listeriosis, which may result in miscarriage, stillbirth, or severe illness in the newborn baby.

Listeria bacteria have also been found in very small amounts in some cook-chill meals so, to be on the safe side, while you are pregnant, always reheat these thoroughly until they are piping hot. Always wash vegetables and salads carefully to remove any soil and dirt which can carry toxoplasmosis infection; this is also the reason why it is also best to make sure that any goat's milk you drink is pasteurised, sterilised or ultra-heat-treated (UHT). Talking of toxoplasmosis - although this isn't really food-related, it's relevant in connection with domestic matters - always wear rubber gloves and take extra care if you have to deal with cat litter.

If you or the baby's father or any previous children have a history of hayfever, asthma, eczema or other allergies, avoiding peanuts and foods containing them (including groundnut oil) in pregnancy and while breast-feeding may reduce the risk of your baby developing a potentially serious allergy to peanuts.

Moderate alcohol consumption during pregnancy is not causing the concern it did a few years ago. However, alcohol does pass through the placenta and directly affects the baby, so the less you drink the better. Latest research suggests that there is no evidence of harm from drinking 2 units of alcohol a day and a maximum of 8 units a week. A unit of alcohol is half a pint (25cl) of beer, lager or cider; a small glass of wine or sherry; a single small measure of spirit or liqueur. It's important that if you do drink, you do so sparingly and don't consume all 8 units at once, at a party, for instance.

Like alcohol, the stimulant caffeine, found in coffee, tea, cocoa and cola-type drinks, also passes through the placenta to the baby. There have been concerns that it might lead to birth defects or miscarriages but studies have failed to give conclusive results.

Obviously, doctors advise against smoking, which is associated with low birth weight and cot death. It appears to have a worse effect later in pregnancy than in the first few weeks so it's never too late to cut down or give up. Details of a helpline for women who are pregnant and want to stop smoking, are at the back of this book.

While you are pregnant, any kind of medication must be considered very carefully and certainly only prescribed by a doctor who knows about your condition. This specifically includes aspirin, paracetamol and cold remedies that may contain them, and also vitamin supplements and recreational drugs.

Although all sweeteners used in food and drink in the UK are said to pose no risk to anyone, including pregnant women, I would also avoid them as they cross the placenta and are eliminated very slowly from foetal tissues.

■ COPING WITH POSSIBLE PROBLEMS IN PREGNANCY

Morning Sickness
When you first become pregnant, you may well feel slightly sick and not much like eating. During these early days you may find that there are only certain foods you want. Some people find milk, milky drinks and yoghurt helpful, while others turn to fresh fruits, salads or wholemeal bread. Herb teas, especially peppermint and camomile can be useful.

For most people this stage only lasts for the first few weeks. If you do find you cannot eat normally, do not fear that your baby is being under-nourished. Only if you are constantly sick and cannot keep anything down is it necessary to see your doctor, for in that case the baby could

23

■ A WEEKS' EASY MENUS FOR THE EARLY DAYS AFTER YOUR BABY'S BIRTH
(Dishes marked * are suitable for freezing)

DAY 1
LUNCH: Felafel* in pitta bread with hummus and salad; fresh fruit or vegetable juice and/or fresh fruit

DINNER: Rigatoni with Mediterranean Sauce with mixed salad with some walnuts; fruit and yoghurt

DAY 2
LUNCH: Very quick lentil soup* with bread, cheese and crudités; fresh juices and/or fruit

DINNER: Roasted Vegetables with cooked brown rice or quinoa; mixed leaf salad; hummus or tahini sauce; nectarines

DAY 3
LUNCH: Left-over Roasted Vegetables with brown rice from previous evening; green salad; fresh juices and/or fruit / or dairy or soya yoghurt

DINNER: Tofu flan* with steamed carrots or mixed salad and mashed potatoes; ripe pears

DAY 4
LUNCH: Left-over Tofu flan; mixed salad; fresh fruit or vegetable juice and/or fresh fruit

DINNER: Quinoa pilaff with sundried tomatoes, raisins and pinenuts* with green salad; baked peaches and yoghurt

DAY 5
LUNCH: Hummus sandwiches; mixed salad; fresh juices and/or fruit with dairy or soya yoghurt

DINNER: Tagliatelle with Broccoli Cream Sauce*; mixed salad; raspberries

DAY 6
LUNCH: Rice and toasted seed salad (see p70) * with tahini dressing or hummus; green salad; fresh fruit or vegetable juice and/or fresh fruit

DINNER: Lentil and Broccoli Gratin* with baked or mashed potatoes and steamed carrots; Baked Apples with raisins or Baked Bananas

DAY 7
LUNCH: Left-over Lentil and Broccoli Gratin with chutney and green salad; fresh fruit or vegetable juice or fruit with a handful of nuts and raisins

DINNER: Tofu Satay; steamed broccoli; Lychee and Kiwi Fruit Salad

Notes on the menus:
— It is helpful to save a portion of the evening meal for your lunch the following day, either to reheat or to eat cold.
— It is assumed that you will take about 600ml/1 pint milk or soya milk during the day, in drinks, snacks, on breakfast cereals, and in main dishes where applicable.
— Desserts are optional, but the ones I've given are relatively simple. Yoghurt or soya yoghurt are included in many of them as a good way of consuming extra milk.

be at risk. Otherwise, just try to make sure that the foods you do eat are as whole and as natural as possible.

Once you know what is happening, you will probably find that you can control the nausea to some extent by having something to eat or drink as soon as you feel that strange, hungry, sick feeling. It is often helpful to avoid fatty foods and to eat little and often. Dry wholemeal toast or crackers might be helpful. You might also try eating a few dates or drinking a little apple or orange juice.

Food Cravings

The tendency to have odd cravings for foods in pregnancy is well known, and, within reason, these do not usually do any harm. If excessive, they may show a lack of some mineral, particularly iron (take medical advice), but minor food cravings are normal and, in my opinion, to be indulged if possible, for they'll pass as the pregnancy progresses.

Heartburn

If you are suffering from heartburn (usually caused by the growing baby pressing against your stomach), it may help if you eat frequent small meals and cut out fatty foods as much as possible.

Constipation

A tendency towards constipation can be eased by increasing your intake of high fibre foods: wholemeal bread, pulses (especially red kidney beans), nuts, fresh vegetables (including potatoes and beetroot), and fruit (especially raspberries). Also, remember to drink plenty of water throughout the day. If you are also suffering from haemorrhoids, try to include buckwheat (see p.93) in your diet because this food contains rutin, a natural remedy for haemorrhoids and also for varicose veins.

Excessive Weight Gain

There is no reason why a vegetarian diet should be any more fattening than a conventional one, but pregnancy is a time when many women find

they gain extra pounds very easily. If you find that your weight is increasing too rapidly, you would be wise to concentrate on the low-calorie high-protein foods, such as cottage and curd cheese, yoghurt, tofu, pulses, wheatgerm and skimmed milk, with liberal amounts of fresh vegetables and fruit. Many people are now questioning the wisdom of restricting weight gain too drastically during pregnancy. I rather go along with this view. Some reserves of fat (but not too many) are helpful when it comes to the demands upon your body of breast-feeding; they can also help you weather the general stresses and strains of the early days with a young baby. And if you breast-feed for at least six months, you will almost certainly find that this extra weight just melts away even though you are, quite rightly, eating more than normal. But you do have to be patient while your food-stores, in the form of body fat, are gradually used up in the production of milk for your baby. Then, with any luck, you'll find you're back to normal; if not, then when breast-feeding is over is the time to adjust your diet a bit, as described above, in order to help you lose those last few pounds.

With all these 'dos' and 'don'ts', and the tests which are now commonplace, it's easy to forget that pregnancy is a perfectly normal, natural, healthy state. You can lose confidence in the ability of the human body to function normally without intervention and to produce healthy, beautiful babies, just as it has done for thousands of years. So, while doing your best to nourish and care for your body, have faith in it and its ability to produce a perfect baby.

■ THINKING AHEAD

A little forethought can make all the difference to how you feel and how you cope in the early days after the birth. If this is your first baby you will probably have little idea how dramatically her arrival will affect you, your partner and your home. At first, the needs of your baby will fully occupy you, to the exclusion of almost everything else. If your baby is anything like the majority, you will also have to put up with many interruptions during the night. And you will be

25

coping with all this, having been through the incredibly intense experience of childbirth, with its enormous demands on you, physically, mentally and emotionally.

For all these reasons, it's worth organising things so that your life is as easy as possible during the first six weeks or so after the birth. Accept all offers of help with housework, washing and shopping. Having a relative or friend to stay, or to pop in for a few hours each day for a week or so after the birth, to deal with the cleaning, washing and cooking, can make such a difference.

Whether or not this is possible, it's worth looking at your home from the point of view of easy cleaning. Remove any unnecessary dust traps like ornaments, for instance, and get an extension lead for the vacuum cleaner so that you can whiz it over several rooms without having to unplug it.

It is not being overly cautious to make a rough meal plan now, perhaps along the lines of the one below, stocking up with the appropriate ingredients and getting some complete dishes - whether home-made or bought - safely stashed away in the freezer. In fact the more complete meals you can get into the freezer before your baby is born, the better. Many of the dishes in this book freeze well. In addition, it's helpful to have some of the following 'freezer basics' for making vegetarian meals quickly and easily:

— homemade sauces for pasta etc: tomato sauce, Mediterranean sauce, broccoli cream sauce, cheese sauce, green lentil sauce, dal sauce. These can be frozen for approximately 8 weeks
— a variety of breads: stock up on a few of your favourite types of bread; basic wholemeal; wholemeal pitta breads and burger buns for quick snacks; ciabatta or granary for a change. Bread can be frozen for approximately 6-8 weeks
— prepared dishes: rice salad with toasted seeds; lentil soup; spinach lasagne; cheese and onion roll; vegetarian minestrone soup; spicy beanburgers; broccoli and lentil gratin; hummus. Prepared dishes can also be frozen for approximately 6-8 weeks

(NB, homemade sauces, bread and prepared dishes are perfectly safe to eat if frozen for longer - even up to 6 months - but the flavour and texture may be impaired)

In addition to stocking the freezer, as your pregnancy draws to a close, you'll want to make sure that your cupboard and refrigerator are well stocked with some of the basics needed for making quick meals.

— grains: brown rice, risotto rice, any other grains you particularly like such as quinoa
— wholemeal flour
— pasta
— canned beans and lentils
— split red lentils
— nuts and seeds - keep them in the freezer
— tahini
— coconut milk or creamed coconut
— tofu: keep in the fridge but don't buy too far in advance as it's nicest when it's as fresh as possible
— oil
— favourite spices and flavourings

You might also like to investigate the possibility of doing your basic food shopping on-line. Some supermarket sites are easier to use than others, but after you've done your first order (which takes about 2 hours), subsequent ones can be done in a jiffy so it's worth getting organised with this before your baby is born.

Your partner or a friend might be willing to prepare some dishes for the freezer or organise meals for just after the birth. Some mums team up with a friend who is also pregnant or has just given birth (about six months behind or ahead of them) and cook extra portions of the family meal to take round to each other for a couple of weeks after the birth.

Coping in the early days

from birth to three months

Whether you've had your baby in hospital or at home, it's a daunting moment when you suddenly realise that the responsibility for the welfare of this demanding and probably unpredictable small person now rests entirely with you. Added to this, you may well still feel tired and perhaps physically battered from the birth and your hormones are in a state of transition, changing from a pregnant to a non-pregnant state and adjusting to breast-feeding.

Do not be surprised, therefore, if you feel fragile and weepy, just when everyone expects you to be feeling thrilled with your baby and on top of the world. This will come, but your body needs time to recover and adapt. Emotionally, too, you need time to think over and relive the birth, and adjust to your new role. Giving birth is a tumultuous experience and both you and your partner need to be able to 'talk it out' during these early post-birth days.

So don't set yourself any target just yet, except that of gradually getting back your strength and helping your baby to settle into a harmonious routine. It's also worth knowing that it takes about six weeks for the milk supply to become firmly established. Once you have been feeding successfully for this length of time, it takes a very great deal to upset things. But until then, this is another reason for making an extra effort to look after yourself by avoiding unnecessary stresses and strains and taking care not to get too tired.

In this context, it's worth remembering that some cultures, for instance the Vietnamese, expect the mother to remain in seclusion for the first month after birth, which I think is a good idea. I think we in the West could learn something from these cultures; we try to be 'superwoman' and feel slightly guilty if we're not 'back to normal' within a few days of the birth. I certainly felt emotionally fragile and vulnerable for at least a month after my babies were born.

■ BEING FLEXIBLE
Babies aren't born with an instinctive knowledge of the difference between night and day, and few

that I have met that have sleeping and eating habits which conform in any way to the idea of 'four-hourly feeds' and the neat little timetables given in old-fashioned baby books. Most new mothers are surprised and puzzled by the frequency with which their baby cries and wants to be picked up and fed: quite different from the mental picture they may have of a baby lying serenely asleep in the cot.

The first few weeks can therefore be somewhat chaotic, and in my opinion you will weather them best - and get the most enjoyment from your baby - if you can adopt a very flexible attitude. Accept that a pattern and routine will emerge, but that you and your baby need to grow into this together and that the process cannot be hurried. I realise that this attitude is easier for people like me who haven't much sense of time, and rather enjoy doing things at odd hours, than for those who like a more organised, orderly existence. But trying to be too orderly and organized with a young baby is nerve-racking for all concerned. It is less harrowing if you can let the baby set the pace and fit your timetable into the baby's, rather than try to make your baby fit yours. Later, as you get used to your baby's pattern, you will find that you can manipulate it to some extent by either waking her for a feed or keeping her going for a bit longer before feeding.

Feeding Your New Baby
Milk is the only food your baby will need during the early days. You will need to decide whether you are going to breast-feed or bottle-feed.

Breast is Best
Health experts agree that breast-milk is the best food for your baby. The Department of Health and the Royal College of Midwives say that, ideally, it's best for babies to be breast-fed exclusively until they are six months old.

Although formula milks are constantly being developed and improved, to make them more like breast-milk, they can never contain exactly the same cocktail of hormones, enzymes and substances to help fight bacterial and viral infections. Breast-milk can also adjust if a baby is premature, alter as your baby grows and her needs change, and even dilute in hot weather to satisfy a baby's thirst. A bottle-feed cannot replace the closeness and skin contact your baby gets when feeding from you.

In addition, once breast-feeding is established, it's much easier and more practical than bottle-feeding. There's no sterilising of equipment, no buying of milk powder, no making up of feeds, no heating up of milk during the small hours of the night, no chance of forgetting the baby's food if you go out for the day.

Breast-feeding also helps your body to return to normal more quickly after the birth, because your uterus contracts when you breast-feed. It may also protect against cancer of the breast, ovaries and cervix. And, if you breast-feed exclusively, it will reduce your chances of conceiving, though it cannot be relied on for contraception without another method. It's important when you're breast-feeding to make sure you're getting enough nutrients – see page 18 for more about this and the healthy snacks you can have to keep your energy up and your milk supply boosted.

You may wonder whether there are any foods that you should avoid while breastfeeding. There are no official recommendations of foods to avoid, although some mums do notice that their babies are particularly 'windy' after they have eaten certain foods (garlic is one that is sometimes mentioned) and so tend to avoid them, but there's no scientific proof. Obviously it's important to eat the most health-giving and nourishing food you can and I believe it's best to choose organic produce whenever possible.

If You Have to Bottle-feed

Whether you breast-feed or bottle-feed, the most important thing is for you to have a relaxed, happy and rewarding feeding relationship with your baby. If you can't breast-feed, or for various reasons choose to bottle-feed, there are compensations. Babies often sleep better after a

bottle-feed because formula milk forms curds in the stomach which makes them feel satisfied for longer. You may also feel less pressurised if other people can help with some of the feeds.

The First Breast-feed

The only preparation you need to make for breast-feeding while you are pregnant is to wash and dry your breasts normally when you have a bath or shower but don't use soap or shower gels which could wash away the natural lubricants. It's also good to get used to handling your breasts so that you don't feel awkward later on.

The baby's sucking reflex is at its strongest in the first few hours after birth, so when your baby is handed to you it is a good idea to put her straight to your breast. If, however, for some reason you feel you cannot do this (because you're too exhausted, too ill or just cannot make yourself), or if you try and the baby does not understand what to do, do not worry. Just try again quietly and gently a little later, perseverance and good support usually lead to success. I was worried when one of my daughters showed absolutely no interest in feeding just after she was born, but she had a feed a few hours later and subsequently proved to be the keenest breast-feeder of all.

Latching On

Do not wash your breasts before you feed. To put your baby to your breast, if you're sitting up (supported by pillows if necessary so that you feel relaxed and comfortable) rest her head on your forearm. Make sure that you're holding her with her body towards you so that she will not have to turn in order to reach your breast.

Position her with her head tipped back slightly so that her chin is close to your breast and her lips are near your nipple: 'chest to chest, chin to breast' is a good maxim. When her lips brush your nipple she will open her mouth really wide, almost as if she is going to yawn. This may take several minutes so be patient. She needs to open her mouth wide so that she takes not just your nipple but also a good mouthful of breast, to protect your nipple from friction so that you do not get sore.

29

If she is latched on properly you will see her jawbone move as she sucks. If not, slide your little finger into the corner of her mouth to break her suction and try again.

Let your baby suck from one side until she comes off of her own accord, then offer the other breast only if necessary. After your baby has finished feeding, dry your breasts carefully. If you have problems with leaking, cover them with a washable or disposable breast pad. Some people suggest putting on some nipple cream or using a spray but this is not advisable as it interferes with the delicate balance of natural secretions. Wash your nipples once a day without using soap, and keep them dry. Cotton bras can help also.

When the Milk Comes In

Giving short feeds as often as your baby will co-operate in the early days will give you both practice. During these early feeds, your baby is getting not milk but colostrum, which helps her to excrete the meconium from her bowel. Meconium is a sticky black waste product which builds up while your baby is in the womb. The actual milk comes in a few days after birth. This might be the second, third or fourth day. The milk usually comes in more quickly with second and subsequent babies, but the timing depends on how much sucking your baby has been able to do. The more you have been able to feed your baby, the more your breasts will have been stimulated, and the quicker the milk will come in, although until it does, the colostrum will supply all that your baby needs.

When the milk does come in you may well find that you are really 'bursting' and the process is rather messy, although giving frequent brief feeds from the beginning will also help to minimise engorgement. Just keep on feeding your baby completely on demand and your supply will quickly adjust to her needs. If you find you have so much milk that it gushes out too quickly, making your baby splutter and choke, you can slow down the flow a little by holding your breast in your fingers, just above the areola, and pushing gently upwards.

In the early days you may find that milk leaks from your breasts between feeds; even hearing the cry of a baby can trigger the 'let down reflex', which brings in the milk, and cause this to happen. A washable or disposable breast pad inside your bra helps, as does wearing dark-coloured tops which do not show up any wet patches too obviously.

Don't let these inconveniences put you off. They will all pass rapidly as you and your baby get used to breast-feeding. Before long, your breasts will shrink back to a much more normal size (even though they are producing large quantities of milk), they will not leak, and the whole process of breast-feeding will become smooth, easy and delightful.

It's best not to be in too much of a hurry to give supplementary bottles. Many mothers do this because they doubt their own ability to produce enough milk. But your body responds to the baby's demand, so if you start to give bottles, the baby takes less milk from you, you produce less so you have to give more bottles and so it goes on. If you really want to breast-feed, just persevere, feed your baby on demand, and trust yourself and nature.

Expressing Milk

If your breasts become very full, they may get so firm that the baby has trouble taking your nipple. If you are engorged, expressing some milk first may make it easier for the baby to latch on. It's also useful to be able to express milk if your baby is born prematurely, so that she can be fed on your milk and, later, so that you can leave milk for her if you have to go out.

To express milk, hold your breast in one hand and use the other to stroke downwards towards the areola. Do this a number of times, to get the milk moving in the ducts. Then support your breast in the palm of your hand, with your thumb about halfway up your breast. Run your thumb down your breast towards the areola, pressing as you do so. Do it gently; don't bruise the tissue. The milk will drip out of the nipple.

If you're doing this simply to rid yourself of excess milk, you can do it over a washbasin. If your milk is being saved to feed your baby, or for the hospital milk bank, then you will need to catch the milk in a sterilised jug or plastic container, cover and refrigerate immediately.

You will never completely empty your breasts because, as they're stimulated, they make more milk; but you need to stop when the milk is only coming out more slowly. If you have to express milk regularly, an electric breast pump is helpful. Manual breast pumps are much cheaper, though not quite as easy to use as the electric ones.

Breast feeding Problems

Most mothers experience a few seconds of discomfort as the baby grasps the breast. After that it passes: it does not last for the whole feed. This sensation is caused by the rush of milk forcing the ducts open. It only happens during the first two or three weeks, and in fact the baby's sucking will help it to pass.

This kind of discomfort is different from the sort which lasts throughout the feed and indicates damage or stress to the surface of the nipple, thought to be caused by faulty positioning of the baby during feeding. This can be very painful, but can heal quickly. Calendula ointment, which you can get at health shops, is a natural and wonderfully soothing and healing ointment. You can also get excellent free advice from the groups listed under Useful Addresses. If you have any problem with breast-feeding, ask for help early, from your midwife, health visitor, from another mother, or one of the groups mentioned.

Winding your Baby

After your baby has finished feeding, hold her up against your shoulder and gently rub or pat her back until she 'burps'. Make sure that she is straight; if she is curled up, her stomach will be squashed and the wind will not be able to come up. Some babies do not swallow much air as they feed, and not all babies need to burp at every feed, so don't worry if nothing happens.

Don't worry either, by the way, if your baby brings up some milk after feeds. This is quite normal and just means she has had more than enough. The only kind of vomiting you need to take notice of, and report to your doctor immediately, is projectile vomiting, when the baby vomits with such force that the vomit shoots across the room. This may indicate a fault in the baby's stomach muscles which can be completely cured by a small operation.

Bottle-feeding

Unless for some reason you are unable to breast-feed, or really loathe the idea of breast-feeding, I think that it's a pity to start bottle-feeding until you have given breast-feeding a really good try. In this case, it's worth remembering that it can take up to six weeks or so to establish breast-feeding, not just ten days or a fortnight, which is what some mothers seem to assume. So do not be in too much of a hurry to give up; do give yourself and your baby time to learn the art. Having tried, there is no reason to feel guilty if you are unable to breast-feed or choose to bottle-feed. It can be a satisfying experience.

For bottle-feeding, you will need six feeding bottles and teats: wide-necked bottles are easier to fill but may cost a bit more. Warm milk provides a perfect environment for bacteria; in addition, even the best formula milk does not contain the antibodies and natural immunity which passes from mother to baby in breast-milk.

So you have to be scrupulous about hygiene when making up feeds, and the feeding bottles and all the equipment you use for measuring and mixing have to be thoroughly washed and sterilised after every use. To do this, you can use cold water with sterilising tablets or liquid, which is the cheapest option; or buy an electric steam steriliser which is convenient and uses no chemicals, or a microwave steriliser which is compact.

It's important to buy a formula milk, which has been specially designed for babies, so that it's as much like human milk as possible. Don't be tempted to use ordinary cow's milk or evaporated milk which are not right for your baby's delicate digestion and could put too much strain on her kidneys. When deciding which type of milk to use, check that it is fortified with the vitamins your baby needs (and which she gets automatically from breast-milk). Also read the making-up instructions to see how easy it is to use.

Soya Formulas

If you're vegan you may wonder about the advisability of using soya baby milks since some concern has been expressed regarding their safety. This is because soya beans contain compounds called isoflavins. The isoflavins are also known as phytoestrogens and they behave like oestrogen, the natural female hormone.

Although the isoflavins are very weak (with 1:1,000 to 1:100,000 the potency of oestrogen) they occur in very high concentrations so people eating soya products take in much higher levels of isoflavins than oestrogen. So, do isoflavins have any ill effects on humans in general and babies in particular?

In adults, rather than increasing oestrogenic activity, isoflavins actually normalise oestrogen levels. So women (such as the Japanese) who include soya products and soya milk in their diets have lower levels of oestrogen in their bloodstream and thus a reduced risk of breast cancer. Conversely, isoflavins will lift the oestrogen level in women who have abnormally low levels of oestrogen in their blood. This raises the issue of what effects isoflavins may have on newborn babies and this is unknown and difficult to judge.

However the consensus of opinion amongst those who have studied this question carefully is that in assessing the possible dangers of using soya milk we need to look at what has happened to all those babies who have been raised on soya milk over the last 20 years. There has not been one human study demonstrating adverse effects (apart from allergic reactions) and there have been literally hundreds of studies demonstrating the positive effects of soya generally.

It's also worth remembering that cow's milk is itself loaded with oestrogen's and that these are not mild ones, derived from plants, but potent oestrogen's from another mammal which may well have some significant effects that have not yet been fully recognised, such as precocious puberty. On the evidence available, it seems that soya milk is a safe food both for babies and adults.

The Soya Milk Information Bureau states:

'Soya formulas are safe for use in babies under one year but they are not the first choice of baby milk and should only be used with good reason after medical and dietetic consultation. In all cases there should be a proven need for a non-dairy baby milk. When a soya-based product is required soya formulas rather than conventional soya milks should be used at least until the child is two years and may be used up to five years.'

Making up formula varies slightly from brand to brand, so read the label. In general, the way to make up feeds is as follows:

— Wash your hands and boil enough water for the number of bottles you intend to make.
— Empty the kettle and put in fresh water - do not use water that has been boiled before, as the concentration of minerals could be too high.
— Put the correct amount into each feeding bottle, using the measure on the side, and let the water cool. (This is quicker than leaving it to cool in the kettle.) Measure the formula using the scoop provided. Don't pack it down, as too much powder can be harmful. Level it off with the back of a knife.
— Add the powder to the bottle, screw on the cap and shake well. Store the bottles in the fridge, and throw away any that are unused after 24 hours.

Some babies like their formula straight from the fridge. Others prefer the bottle warmed in a bottle warmer or jug of hot water for a few minutes.

To bottle-feed, cradle your baby in the crook of your arm so that she is cosy and close to you. When practical, open your shirt so that she can feel your warm skin. Gently touch the baby's cheek nearest to you; as she turns towards you, pop the teat into her mouth. Make sure you tilt the bottle well so that the milk fills the teat-end of the bottle and no air can get in, which could give her colic. (Anti-colic teats are available from the chemist.) Pull on the bottle a little as your baby sucks, to keep up the suction. After your baby has finished the feed, 'burp' her as described on p.31.

Coping During the Day

In these early days your baby will be happiest and you will probably cope best if you pick her up when she cries and offer a feed. Although this is the most natural thing to do, for some reason most people – and I was the same myself – have the feeling that their baby ought to sleep for longer and conform roughly to the ideal of four hourly feeds, each followed by a peaceful sleep!

Then there are plenty of well-meaning people only too ready to tell you that you're spoiling your baby by picking her up, that your baby is only crying because 'she wants you to pick her up', and that 'the baby needs to exercise her lungs by crying'. But you cannot 'spoil' such a tiny baby, and her lungs do not need any exercise other than that which she gets every time she breathes. And yes, your baby probably is crying because she wants you to pick her up. But if you think about it, that, too, is natural, considering how close your baby has been to you for nine months. The physical closeness between you both needs to continue, easing away very gently and gradually over the weeks and months.

Feeding on Demand

When your baby cries, assume that she wants feeding, and put her to your breast, even if the last feed was as recent as half an hour ago. This frequent feeding will, as I have already said, stimulate your breasts to produce more milk, thus increasing your supply. It's because breast-feeding depends on this supply-and-demand system that breast-milk, though a perfect food, does not

sustain your baby for as long as formula milk. Breast-fed babies need feeding more often than those who are on formula, which I see as nature's way of ensuring that the transition from womb to independence is a very gradual one.

If you get a situation where it is essential for your baby to sleep for a period of three or four hours, for your own sanity, the preservation of your relationship, or some other reason, giving your baby 50-75ml/2-3fl oz of formula milk from a bottle (if she will take a bottle) will probably ensure this. It can also be a good idea to give your baby an occasional bottle of, say, boiled water, to get her used to taking a bottle. But if you're serious about breast-feeding, this is best kept as a last resort, rather than becoming a habit.

Of course, babies do cry for reasons other than wanting to be cuddled and fed. As the days go by you will get to understand what the various cries mean and when, for instance, your baby is crying with irritable exhaustion just prior to falling asleep. But at this stage, when your baby is so tiny and you are trying to establish the feeding, I think it is best to try a cuddle and a feed first, before she gets so upset that she finds it impossible to feed.

Remember that you can't overfeed a breast-fed baby and in many parts of the world feeding continues virtually all the time, with the contented baby carried in a sling at her mother's breast, able to have a little suck whenever she feels the need. It may well be the comfort of sucking, and the knowledge of your closeness, which your baby needs, rather than food. If you have a very 'cuddly' baby, you might find it helpful to use a sling.

Comforting your Baby

If you feel that your baby is unduly restless, check that she is the right temperature. Being small, babies lose and gain heat quickly and their hands are not always a good guide to their body temperature. A tiny baby's need for fresh air is greatly overstated; don't let her get cold by being outside in a pram or buggy for long periods of time; a normal airy room can supply all the 'fresh air' she needs. On the other hand, your baby can get overheated in a warm room if you pile on too many blankets, so you need to be vigilant to get it just right. If you're worried about whether your baby is too warm, slip your fingers inside her clothing and feel her chest; if it's clammy, it means she's too hot.

Something else which can have a soothing effect if your baby is restless is to wrap a shawl firmly around her, then tuck in the covers firmly and cosily when you put her down in the cot. This gives her the feeling of being securely held. When your baby no longer needs to be so firmly tucked up, she will let you know by wriggling and kicking off the covers.

If you have a very 'sucky' baby and find the almost constant feeding too much to cope with, you might consider giving your baby a dummy. Most new parents don't give their baby a dummy when it would be very helpful, for example for colic or during fretful evenings, because they are terrified the baby will become addicted and they will never be able to get the dummy away. But your baby will give up the dummy of her own accord when she is less desperate for comfort-sucking.

A dummy can be a great comfort to mother and baby alike. I certainly recommend them as long as they're not used so excessively that they prevent the baby from getting all the physical comfort and cuddles she needs, and the frequent feeds which help to establish breast-feeding in the early days.

If you do use a dummy, keep it scrupulously clean by placing it in a steriliser when your baby is not using it. Never put any form of sweetener on the dummy and do not give your baby a dummy containing fruit juice or other liquid. These will interfere with her demand for breast-milk and may have a detrimental effect on her teeth.

Don't feel that you have to give your baby a bath every day. A daily bath is fine if you have the time and if your baby likes it. But many newborn babies dislike their bath and this, combined with a new mother's natural apprehension and awkwardness, can make the bath a worrying time for both. Your baby will be fine as long as she is 'topped-and-tailed'. This means gently washing her face and hands, washing her bottom and putting on a clean nappy and clothes as necessary.

Lively Babies

Some babies just seem to be born lively and if you happen to have one of these you will not get much peace. She certainly will not sleep for as long as other babies and she will want to see what is going on.

The way to cope with a baby like this is to let her be wherever you are, in the midst of the household clamour. Put your baby, where she can see you, in one of those little rocking cradle chairs, baby car seat or convertible reclining chair, or prop her up in her cot or in a chair. Make sure that she is firmly supported with cushions and cannot slip.

Talk to your baby often – the sound of your voice will be reassuring – and make sure there is always plenty for her to look at. Coloured mobiles are a good idea and are quite inexpensive to make. You can use coloured card cut into shapes or small colourful objects strung up from a hook in the ceiling.

An alternative is to stretch a piece of rope across the baby's pram, like a washing line, and peg or tie on to it different items such as brightly coloured tissue paper, a string of bells, a piece of bright ribbon. Change the objects often to keep the baby's interest. Babies also like looking at coloured birthday cards or pictures pushed down the sides of the cot and pram.

A musical box is often a great success with tiny babies. You could also buy a recording of simulated womb noises which has a calming effect on a restless baby. I believe a recording of an automatic washing machine, with its whirls and gurgles, has a similar effect; or, easier still, simply put the baby near the washing machine!

However hard you try you will probably get one of those days when your baby never seems to stop demanding and you feel at your wits' end. This is the time when it's so marvellous if you have a kind neighbour who understands this desperate feeling and will take your baby, immediately, for half an hour to give you a breather. But if you haven't such a neighbour, remember that ten minutes of crying never hurt any baby. Put her out of earshot, make yourself a drink, and set the timer for ten minutes. Then relax. You'll be surprised how different you feel when the timer goes and you return to your baby.

When you're struggling with a difficult baby who is lively, never sleeps and cries easily with frustration or boredom, it's sometimes helpful to remember that all the characteristics you find such hard work have a flip side: aggression = drive; obstinacy = perseverance; liveliness = interest in life, and so on. Babies who are very hard work become children who never cease to amaze and delight you. It's tempting to think 'oh for a dim baby who sleeps' but is that what you really want?

Coping During the Evening

One of the most difficult times with a young baby is in the evening when many seem to have a fretful period just when you are tired and longing to have an hour or so to yourself. This, in my opinion, is where demand-feeding is such a help.

The way I coped with this difficult time, which I had with all three of my daughters, was to get in a good supply of interesting books and magazines, make myself a soothing drink, sit in a comfortable chair with my feet up, and let the baby feed while I relaxed.

It is a demanding stage and if you adopt my policy it does mean that your evenings are a write-off and it's useless to plan any social life, so you'll need the understanding and support of the rest of the family. But though it seems hard to believe at the time, this stage passes very quickly - within a few weeks - and you will probably look back on it with some nostalgia in the future.

You may well feel that there is not much milk left at the end of the day but, as I have explained, your baby's sucking action will stimulate the milk so the more she sucks, the more there will be. If, on the other hand, you think your baby is wanting to suck for comfort, rather than for food, you might well find that a dummy could be the answer. I know it's not aesthetically pleasing, but it could make all the difference to your evenings. If you think your baby is wanting to suck because she is hungry, and that the problem is that you're short of milk in the evenings, it is better to try to increase your own supply if you wish to continue with breast-feeding, rather than to start giving supplementary feeds from a bottle.

Increasing Your Supply of Milk

— Feed your baby more often
— Check your baby's position to make sure she's stimulating your breasts and is able to get all your milk
— Let her finish at one breast, then offer the other
— Check that you are eating and drinking enough; this is not the time to worry about dieting or losing weight - that will happen naturally as the weeks go by. Plenty of cooked brown rice - at least 450g/1lb a day, and hummus or tahini dip is one successful mother's tip for giving her milk supply a boost, see page 71-2
— Make sure you are getting as much rest as you can; accept all offers of help
— Remember that it takes several days to increase your milk supply (you won't see much change in less than 48 hours), so keep on trying for at least two weeks before you judge the results

Quick Nutritious Snacks for Breast-feeding Mums

During breast-feeding your need for extra nutrients continues pretty much as it did when you were pregnant although now you will need more protein and calories. If you're vegan make sure you're getting enough B12 enriched foods. Boosting your normal meals with one or two nourishing snacks during the day will ensure that you (and your baby) are well nourished. At first it's hard even to find time to make breakfast or lunch for yourself so having several good-quality

35

snacks during the day could be more practical. Here are some suggestions:

— A handful of mixed nuts and seeds with dried fruit
— A bowl of Very Quick Lentil Soup with wholemeal bread, see page 81
— Lentil dal with brown rice
— Wholemeal peanut butter, tahini, hummus or cheese sandwich with salad
— Hummus and pitta bread
— Tahini Dip or Hummus with vegetables, see page 71-2
— Banana shake: whiz a banana in some milk or soya milk (B12 and calcium-fortified) with 2 teaspoons blackstrap molasses and 50g/2oz ground almonds.
— A bowl of creamy porridge (made with half water, half milk or soya milk) topped with flaked almonds or ground hazel nuts
— Quick brown rice salad: mix chopped red or green pepper, onion, tomato with cooked brown rice and some toasted pumpkin or sesame seeds; or topped with Gomasio or tahini dressing
— Red Kidney Bean and Avocado Salad with wholemeal or pitta bread, see page 75
— Felafel with salad and tahini dressing in pitta bread
— Any of the iron-rich snacks on pp. 21-2
— Nourishing Fruit Cake, Parkin or Molasses Flapjacks, see p112-5
— Bought veggieburger or Spicy Beanburger in a wholemeal bun with tahini dressing

Evening Colic

In the evening very many babies seem to have a restless, fretful period, when they cry more than usual, and often parents think that the reason for this is colic. When a baby has colic (which often does not start until she is about a month old), she appears to be in real pain, drawing her knees up to her stomach, crying and sobbing uncontrollably. Nothing seems to comfort her for any length of time; doctors do not know the cause of the problem and there seems to be little that they can do to help.

Gripe water is sometimes helpful or you can make a dill water by steeping a teaspoonful of lightly crushed dill seeds in a couple of tablespoons of boiling water, cooling and straining. A dummy can also be helpful. Warmth, from a well-wrapped hot water bottle, put near (but not on top of) the baby's tummy, can also help. And some mothers find merbentyl, from the doctor, works for true colic. But one of the troubles with real colic is that there seems to be so little you can do. You keep trying things, and these seem to work for a short time, then the screaming and drawing-up of the legs starts again and you're at a loss as to what to do.

If your baby really has got colic, it is not because of something you're doing wrong. It's just one of those inexplicable things, and you will have to face the fact that you're going to have very difficult evenings for a few weeks, whilst giving her what comfort and reassurance you can. This is extremely taxing and demanding, and it will help if you and your partner can take turns to cope alternately with your baby throughout the evening. The only really comforting thing I can say is that colic rarely lasts for more than eight weeks and invariably stops, usually quite suddenly, by the time the baby is three to four months old.

Coping at Night

When you put your baby down for the night, it's a good idea to try and create a different atmosphere from daytime sleeps. Put your baby in her cot in the bedroom; make sure that the room is warm and dark, with perhaps just a low light, so that you do not have to switch on more light and risk waking her when you go to bed yourself or when you're dealing with night feeds.

Making Night Feeds Easy

Unless you are very lucky, once you do finally get to sleep you will probably be awakened at least once during the night. However, breast-feeding does make the night-time feeds relatively easy to cope with, and if you can manage to feed the baby while she is still sleepy the chances are that you will both fall asleep again very quickly.

36

So don't let your baby cry for any length of time; have her near you, if possible right by your bed so that you only have to reach over and pick her up. You can then feed her easily, almost in your sleep, and both go back to sleep again quickly.

Unless you have a very fussy baby, most experienced mothers agree that it is much better not to try and change a nappy in the night unless it is obviously causing discomfort. If you feed quickly and then put your baby straight back into the cot without messing about with creams and nappies, you will both have a better chance of getting back to sleep again.

If you go along with your baby's needs for night feeds, you will find that, just like the day, a pattern gradually emerges. The time between feeds will grow longer. You may find that you can manipulate the time of the night feeds by waking your baby for a feed just before you go to sleep, so that then, with any luck, you can get an unbroken sleep during the early part of the night.

Your baby

from three to six months

Gradually you'll find the chaos and unpredictability of the early baby days pass. You and your baby will evolve a harmonious routine, and she will respond increasingly to you and begin to take a lively interest in the world around her. Babies begin to be fun at around this age and there are various things you can do to entertain your baby and help her to develop mentally.

Research has shown that the more time you spend playing with and talking to your baby, the more quickly she will develop and the more intelligent she is likely to be. Looking after a baby is certainly a great deal more interesting, rewarding and enjoyable if you have some ideas for stimulating and playing with her.

Entertaining Your Baby

Your baby will still enjoy all the things described on p.34: coloured pictures on the walls beside the cot or pushed down the sides of the cot and pram (well secured, or she will grab and eat them as she gets older); coloured mobiles to look at; a musical box to listen to.

In addition, when your baby is around two to three months old, she will enjoy being able to reach out and touch a fluffy ball or rattle suspended from the pram hood or from a piece of dowelling lashed across the cot. Those suction rattles which you can buy to stick to the highchair or the wall beside the cot are also great fun for your baby, as is a 'mobile gym', which consists of various toys for her to push and pull, mounted on a plastic bar that you tie across the cot.

From about three months babies begin to enjoy exploring things with their hands. They like to touch a rattle, a string of wooden beads or cotton reels or a bunch of keys. Give your baby plenty of different objects to handle and study, varying the shapes and textures: a piece of soft material, a small furry toy, some crackly shiny paper rolled into a ball, tissue paper to handle and tear, small empty cardboard boxes and plastic bottles, pieces of sponge, empty egg boxes, rattles made

by putting some dried beans or lentils into a plastic container with a firmly secured lid.

Again, watch for eating; the baby son of a friend of mine used to eat his older sisters' comics and they would come out in his nappy still readable! And I have vivid memories of one of my babies eating handfuls of small pebbles on the beach. I did not realise she had actually swallowed any until I saw what came through in her nappy!

A baby this age will also enjoy playing with your kitchen utensils; a plastic bowl is fun to fill with table tennis balls and, a little later on, saucepans are great to bang with a wooden spoon.

From the age of about three months, as soon as she can hold her head unsupported, your baby can be put into a baby bouncer. This is a little fabric harness attached to a piece of springy rubber, which fastens to a hook in the ceiling, or to a clip over the door frame. As your baby puts a toe on the ground, she will bounce. She will get a great deal of pleasure from bouncing several times a day - and you will be free for a few minutes to get on with something nearby.

Interacting with Your Baby

If yours is a lively baby, you'll be used to having her beside you in her little rocking chair or car seat. All babies will now need this opportunity and will watch happily as you go about your tasks.

Continue to talk to your baby frequently and repeat the sounds which she makes to you. She will love the rhythm of songs and rhymes and will soon respond to games of 'peep-bo', and action rhymes, such as 'pat-a-cake', 'this little piggy went to market' and 'round and round the garden'. Nursery rhyme books and tapes are useful for jogging rusty memories. Your baby will also love brightly coloured picture books.

During this period (between three and six months) your baby will learn to roll over; to sit unsupported for a few seconds and to prepare to crawl. She will love to pull herself up on your

39

knee and bounce about, supported by your body and reassured by your closeness. You can encourage your baby's physical development by letting her lie on a rug in a warm room or sunny garden with the minimum of clothing, protected as necessary by sun block.

Although they're demanding, babies at this stage can be enormously rewarding and fun. The more you cuddle, talk to and play with your baby, the more you will get out of the relationship, and the quicker she will develop. Giving your baby this close attention is not 'spoiling'; it is helping her to develop as fully as possible.

Some mothers seem to enjoy all this naturally; others find themselves distraught with boredom and frustration, resenting and begrudging every demand. Because they're emotionally drained by the effort of meeting their baby's increasing needs, they hold back, trying to keep something in reserve. The baby soon senses this and becomes more demanding as a result. So a vicious circle begins.

If this is a problem for you, I can only say that, paradoxically, the more quickly and fully you meet your baby's demands, the more contented and 'easy' she will be and the more chance you'll both have of being reasonably happy. I strongly advise this course of action, though you may receive advice to the contrary, such as 'you'll spoil the baby', or 'the baby mustn't be taught to think she can have everything she wants'.

I do not agree with these statements and in my experience the reverse is true, as I have explained above. The more certain your baby is of having her needs met, the less anxious and demanding she will become. She will learn from an early age to have a basic confidence in the goodness of life and the expectation that her emotional needs will be met. In any case, a baby of this age is far too young to be able to use her 'power' over you in a calculating way; she is just aware of her needs – for food, comfort, stimulation, love – and that you are the person who will satisfy them.

Looking After Yourself

I personally found I coped best if I considered my baby to be my full-time job during the day, not planning to do anything else except absolutely essential shopping and cooking, and the minimum of necessary cleaning. Then I would look forward to an hour or so of my own in the evening when she was in bed. I certainly found it helpful to line up plenty of activities to keep her happy and amused during the day.

It can also be a very great help to get out and meet other mothers who are in a similar position. Coffee mornings, such as those run on a local basis by the National Childbirth Trust (see Useful Addresses), provide social contact which can be such a morale-booster at this time. I certainly found this to be so, as it is comforting and therapeutic to be able to swap experiences and realise you're not alone in what you're going through. Teaming up with another mother so that you each take it in turns to look after both babies on a regular basis can also be most helpful. It's less emotionally draining to look after two babies for, say, a couple of hours, knowing that later you will get a couple of hours to yourself.

It's important to make sure you're eating enough to keep your energy levels up during this period. Even if you haven't time for proper meals during the day, try to have regular nutritious snacks such as a tub of yoghurt or soya yoghurt, a banana, a pot of hummus with some bread, a handful of nuts and dried fruit or any kind of nutritious snack as described on page 22.

Going Back to Work

Going back to work doesn't have to mean the end of breast-feeding. At the very least you could fit in a cosy feed early in the morning before you leave, to bind you both together before the separation of the working day. Then when you return in the evening you can greet your baby with another feed, helping you to readjust to motherhood; and you can go on feeding your baby during the evening (and in the night as necessary), as much as you wish.

Many working mothers find that their babies wake more for feeds during the night after they have returned to work which is pretty exhausting after a hard day's work. You can take your baby into bed with you and feed her while you are lying down. This is perfectly safe as long as neither partner has had a sedative or alcohol, but it is not advisable if you (or your partner) are very overweight or so exhausted that you're likely to sleep very deeply.

For daytime feeds you can express milk for your baby to have while you are away, or arrange for your baby to have formula milk, or if you work close to home perhaps your baby could be brought to you for feeds, or you might try a combination of all of these possibilities. It will depend on the age of your baby and how far away you work as well as what feels right for you. Only you can decide.

If you express milk while away from home, it must be kept cool, preferably in a fridge. Milk, which you express at lunchtime, could be used the next day. Breast-milk freezes well and will keep for about 4-6 weeks, so you can build up a milk bank. Remember to sterilise all the equipment you use and label the milk with the date. Defrost the milk quickly by standing it in warm water just before you use it. Throw out any that is left over after the feed. Freezing breast-milk isn't ideal because it changes composition as the baby grows, so don't keep larger stocks than necessary.

If your decision involves fewer feeds, give your body time to adjust so that your breasts don't feel uncomfortably full when you are at work. Decide which feeds you will be dropping and stop them, one by one, over a few weeks leading up to your return to work. Let your body adjust to one less feed before dropping another. Many women find themselves getting tearful during this weaning stage - another reason to take things slowly.

If your decision involves bottle-feeds, whether of formula or your own expressed milk, you will need to start getting your baby used to taking a feed from a bottle in good time. She may need several goes to get the hang of it and may take it better from someone else, as she associates you with breast-milk. Keep offering gently, without pressure, and she will probably accept. If she doesn't, she can be fed from a spoon during the day before four months and from a feeder cup after that.

Teething

Towards the end of this six-month period the first tooth or teeth may appear. The timing does vary a good deal, with some babies remaining toothless until around a year, so do not worry if your baby's half birthday passes without any sign of a tooth. Babies often have some discomfort when cutting their teeth, more especially with the back teeth, which appear during their second year, than with the first front teeth. Nevertheless your baby may find it comforting to chew on a teething ring which should be kept sterilised when not in use.

Incidentally, you don't need to stop breast-feeding when your baby's teeth appear. Strangely enough, these do not hurt. This is because your baby's mouth is filled by your nipple and the areola around it, and so her jaws are open, not closed. Sometimes your baby may inadvertently bite at the end of a feed, after she has finished sucking and when she is just 'playing' with your breast. Prevent this by removing the breast as soon as your baby has finished feeding; she will quickly learn not to bite.

If your baby is old enough you could try giving her some cold foods such as yoghurt or apple purée from the fridge, which might ease the pain. You could rub 'teething jelly' on the gums; there's no evidence these actually work though the pressure from your finger applying the jelly may be soothing. Some paediatricians recommend giving a small dose of a child's painkiller - ask your doctor or pharmacist - but on no account give aspirin or rub it into the gums because it can be dangerous for young children.

41

Weaning Your Baby

Weaning, or getting your baby to switch from an all-milk diet to one that includes solid foods, is a process many mothers view with some apprehension. I felt that way myself; if anything it's worse for us vegetarian mothers, who may not know which vegetarian foods are suitable for a baby and may be further unsettled by anxious friends and relatives. However, the weaning process is really a very simple one, and most babies accomplish it amazingly smoothly. Parents can be reassured that a vegetarian diet can offer all the nourishment a baby needs for growth and development. This is how the weaning process might go:

When Your Baby is Four to Six Months Old

You can give your baby a little fresh, unsweetened fruit juice, diluted half-and-half with boiled, cooled water. Apple juice is the best choice because it is less likely to cause an allergic reaction than orange juice. Give this fruit juice, diluted with a little boiled, cooled water, initially from a teaspoon, in the middle of the morning or afternoon. As soon as your baby gets used to taking it in this way, try giving it from a normal cup (not a mug with a feeder lid). This is an excellent way of introducing your baby to a cup. Your baby will be able to drink from a feeder cup at about six months. It's a good idea for her to be able to use both a feeder cup and an ordinary cup. Apart from this juice, continue with breast-feeding or bottle-feeding in the normal way.

Breast-milk supplies all that your baby needs (including vitamin C) for the first six months of life. So if your baby is happy and thriving, there is no need to think about introducing any solids until she is six months old. If, however, after four months your baby does not seem fully satisfied with milk, you might try giving a first taste of food – but don't start before four months. (The danger of introducing solids early is that your baby's immature digestive system cannot readily cope with the food, and so the likelihood of an allergic reaction is increased.)

First Foods

The first spoonfuls are really just to get your baby used to the taste and feel of solid food. Do not think of them as a real source of nourishment at this stage. Your baby still needs milk feeds for that and also for the emotional satisfaction of sucking.

Half a teaspoonful of a fruit or vegetable purée is best for your baby's first taste of solid food. Traditionally cereals were always the first solid food given to babies. However, wheat is now advised against, as this can cause allergies if given too early. Baby rice is fine but be sure to get a plain one rather than one that's flavoured and sweetened. However, for a first taste, I don't think you can beat fresh fruit or vegetable purées.

Use a flat teaspoon and give the first taste at one of the main milk feeds corresponding to breakfast, lunch or dinner, whichever is the most convenient for you. If you are planning to go back to work but want to continue breast-feeding, start giving the solids at lunchtime, for this will eventually become the first meal at which your baby gives up a breast-feed and just has solids.

Whether you give the first taste of solid food before or after the milk feed is up to you, or perhaps, more to the point, up to your baby. But generally speaking, it's better to give solids before the milk feed if you can so that, as you gradually increase the quantity of solids, your baby will be satisfied with these and forget about the milk feed. However, there is no point in trying to give solids if your baby is hungry, wanting comfort and crying for a feed. Better to let her feed first and then give the taste of solids at the end.

Be prepared for the fact that your baby may well spit out your lovingly prepared offerings. Don't worry and don't take it personally. She is not depending on this food for nourishment at this stage. Try again another day, persisting gently; there is no hurry. As your baby gets used to the flavour, you can gradually increase the quantity so that after a few weeks she is having perhaps two tablespoonfuls of food at a time. Increasing the quantity gradually also gives your baby's

42

digestive system plenty of time to become used to coping with solid food.

Allergies

Many mothers worry about possible allergic reactions when they introduce their babies to new foods. Actually allergies are quite rare and where they do occur they are usually inherited, so you will know in advance if they are likely. Delaying the introduction of solid foods until your baby is at least four months old, or preferably six months, makes the risk of an allergic reaction less likely because her digestive system is more able to cope.

Foods most likely to cause allergies are milk and dairy products, eggs, nuts, sugar, chocolate, oranges, wheat and foods containing gluten.

Foods least likely to cause an allergic reaction are rice, oats, root and leafy vegetables, apples and pears, dried fruit, beans and pulses.

Signs of an allergic reaction are rashes and swelling of the eyes, lips and face, sickness; diarrhoea; eczema; hayfever and asthma.

Many so called allergies are simply food intolerance's which disappear as babies get older, usually by the time they are about two years old. Although some allergies, particularly to nuts and dairy products, can last for life.

If you have a family history of asthma, eczema, hay fever or food allergies, the Department of Health recommends that you should avoid all peanuts and peanut products until your child is 3 years old. Also be aware that some baby products have traces of peanut oil (sometimes called arachide) in their production and studies have shown that this can also lead to peanut allergies.

Whether or not you have a history of allergies, asthma and eczema in your family, it's a good idea to try your baby on the same food for at least four days before trying another, so that you can be sure there are no adverse effects. Watch your baby carefully, and if all is well, try her on something else.

■ FOODS FOR WEANING AND HOW TO PREPARE THEM

Carrot

Scrape carrot and boil it in a little unsalted water until tender; purée with enough of the cooking water to get a soft consistency. Start by giving $1/2$ teaspoon before or after the midday or evening milk feed.

Swede, parsnip, sweet potato

Make like carrot purée. These sweet roots, parsnip and sweet potato in particular are good for mixing with other vegetables, particularly leafy green vegetables, to make them more acceptable.

Apple

Use sweet apples only, not tart ones that require added sweetening. Peel, core, and slice apple; cook in 2-3 tablespoons water until tender; purée, adding a little extra boiled water if necessary to get a soft consistency. Or use raw, see below.

Pear

Make like apple purée, using sweet pears. Or use raw, see below.

Banana

Choose very ripe bananas. Peel. Remove the seeds with the point of a knife if you like. Mash flesh thoroughly with a fork, adding a little cooled boiled water if necessary to get a soft consistency.

Courgette

Cut off the ends. Cut into small pieces, cook in a minimum of unsalted water until tender. Purée with enough cooking water to get a soft consistency.

Pumpkin, squash

Peel; remove the seeds. Cut the flesh into pieces and cook in a little boiling water until tender. Purée.

43

Tomato

Equally suitable either raw or cooked. Sieve cooked tomato to remove the seeds. Or scald and peel raw tomato, cut out the core, then mash. (You can remove the seeds if you like, but the jelly around them is a valuable source of soluble fibre.)

Grated apple or pear

Choose sweet apples and well-ripened pears. Peel and grate finely, or simple mash pear if very ripe.

Peaches, apricots, nectarines, sweet cherries, plums, mangoes, papaya, kiwi fruit

Choose really ripe fruit. Remove the skin and stones; mash the flesh thoroughly.

Avocado

Cut in half. Scoop out and mash a little of the flesh, adding a few drops of boiled water to soften if necessary.

Broccoli, cauliflower, Brussels sprouts, green cabbage

Wash and trim. Cook in a minimum of unsalted water until tender enough to mash. Purée with a little of the cooking water. (Cooked cabbage and sprouts can create intestinal gas; if this is a problem, mix with another vegetable purée, such as carrot, parsnip or sweet potato – these sweet flavours also make the purée more acceptable.)

Spinach

Wash thoroughly, remove the stems, and shred the leaves. Cook in a saucepan without extra water until spinach is tender. Purée and maybe mix with carrot etc as above. (Don't give more than once or twice a week since the oxalic acid content affects the body's absorption of some minerals.)

Dried apricots, prunes, pears, peaches, apples

Wash, then cover with boiling water and soak overnight. Next day, simmer until tender. Remove stones from prunes. Purée the fruit. (Some can have rather a laxative effect.)

Baby rice cereal

This is best as a first cereal because it is the least likely to cause allergic reactions. Choose one fortified with additional iron and B vitamins, but avoid sweetened and flavoured varieties. Make up with liquid according to directions on the package.

Potatoes, sweet potatoes

Scrub. Bake, or boil in unsalted water. Scoop potato out of skin and mash. A little very finely grated cheese, curd cheese, cottage cheese, yoghurt, tofu, milk or soya milk can be added; also very finely chopped green vegetables, such as watercress or raw spinach leaves.

Sweetcorn, peas, green beans

Boil until tender; purée. Fresh or frozen are fine; canned are not advised because of the added salt and sugar.

Muesli

Buy a mix without sugar and other additives, or make your own from oats, nuts and raisins, then grind to a powder. Moisten with water, fruit juice or plain yoghurt. Sprinkle with wheatgerm and mix well. Powdered nuts or seeds or grated apple or pear can be added.

Wholemeal bread

From six months onwards, a little crustless bread can be added to vegetable purées. The bran in 100% wholemeal bread and flour is too laxative for some babies; an 81-85% bread (preferably with added wheatgerm, for extra iron) is often a better choice for babies under two years old.

Baby pasta shapes

Useful for adding to vegetable purées to make a more substantial mixture. You can buy special pasta for babies, but it's cheaper and just as good to use tiny pasta shapes, which are normally sold to put into soup.

Preparing and Freezing Babyfood

— Although it is impractical to sterilise all your kitchen equipment when you are preparing babyfood, it is important to be scrupulous about hygiene, especially in the early days

— Dip your baby's spoon in a little boiling water to sterilise it before giving her juice or boiled water

— Sterilise with feeding bottle steriliser any plastic or glass bowls that you are using to prepare her food, and the little dish, cup or plate on which you put your baby's first tastes of solid food

— If you are freezing little portions of babyfood for use later, which saves much time, make sure that the containers are sterilised. Ice cube trays are useful for freezing the small quantities that you will need. If you prepare some of cooked and puréed vegetables say, and some of cooked baby pasta shapes, you can then mix and match them as required later

— Once the food is frozen, remove the cubes from the container and store them in clean polythene bags, carefully labelled with the contents and date

— Make sure that your freezer will freeze food to 0°F/-18°C or below in 24 hours. Defrost the food quickly and throw away any that is left over: do not re-freeze

— Pure fruit and vegetable purées will keep for about six months in the freezer; any that have milk or eggs in them are best used within about six weeks

Suggested Feeding Pattern, from Four to Six Months
— On waking: Breast/bottle-feed
— Breakfast: Breast/bottle-feed
— Mid-morning: Diluted fruit juice from spoon or cup (or give this drink mid-afternoon)
— Lunch: $1/2$-2 teaspoons fruit or vegetable purée; Breast/bottle-feed
— Mid-afternoon: Diluted fruit juice from spoon or cup (unless this was given in the morning)
— Dinner: Breast/bottle-feed
— Before bed: Breast/bottle-feed

45

Your baby

from six to twelve months

During this period your baby will sit up unaided and also begin to crawl; it is an exciting time of rapid physical development. You can encourage the crawling process by putting your baby down on her tummy on the floor, preferably unrestricted by a nappy. If you place a desirable object a little way in front of her, she will soon learn to get to it by crawling forward.

It has been found that the crawling phase is very important for a baby's intellectual development, so do not be in a hurry to get her walking. For this reason it is not a good idea to put your baby into one of those 'walkers' which supports her in a standing position and allows her to propel herself around the room without crawling.

Keeping Your Baby Safe

Once your baby begins to crawl competently, nothing will be safe. For your own peace of mind, and the happiness of both your baby and yourself, it's a good idea to take a look at your home with new eyes, removing everything that can be tipped, broken or pulled.

Your baby will want to be playing around on the floor wherever you are, so it's worth taking the time to make these areas safe. Ensure that:

— there are no loose electric wires and that the open power points are safe, by covering them with plug guards
— fires are securely guarded
— scissors and other sharp instruments are out of reach
— bottles of cleaning fluid, medicines and alcoholic drinks are locked away
— the stairs are blocked off
— you use mainly the back burners on your cooker if your baby is playing around by you while you're cooking
— that hot drinks are out of reach of children
— be careful of sharp corners on furniture
— if you have glass doors you can now buy a protective film which goes over the glass, strengthening it and holding the glass together if it shatters

It takes a bit of an effort to do all this, but is worthwhile because once it is done you can relax and let your baby race around and explore in safety while you get on with things.

Put your baby in old, comfy clothes so that she can get as grubby as she likes. The more unrestricted she is, the better for her development. For this reason it's not a good idea to leave a baby in a playpen for long periods of time (though a playpen can be useful for short periods, to provide a brief respite from being 'on guard' all the time - long enough to answer the phone or drink a cup of tea, for instance).

In general, however, it's not easy for a baby to learn to be an enquiring, hopeful and enterprising adult if her efforts to explore are frustrated or, worst of all, rewarded with a slap. A baby of this age is too young to understand the meaning of punishment and will just be puzzled that the person to whom she looks for comfort and love has suddenly lashed out and hurt her.

Of course, however carefully you 'baby-proof' your home, there will inevitably be times when she will get something she mustn't have, or manage to open a drawer which had hitherto been beyond her. When removing the forbidden treasures, it saves a great deal of hassle and upset if you can divert with an alternative: 'You mustn't have that, but here's something that's just as much fun.'

If there are certain things in the house which you do not want your toddler to touch, by all means explain this to her simply, but you will have to do so over and over again. It's unrealistic to expect a baby of this age to remember, or to override her own will/need/desire; she is incapable of this until she is coming out of toddlerhood. Until then, her will and yours may coincide, but she is not capable of doing something to please you, or to annoy you. You really can't expect a baby or toddler to be aware of the consequences of her actions.

Hygiene

Once your baby is crawling around you may wonder about hygiene, especially as her presence means you're probably not able to clean the house as thoroughly as you'd like. Yet, as long as basic standards of hygiene are maintained, your baby will be fine. Keep the food-preparation areas of the house clean, also the bathroom, and keep pet food (which, like any food, can harbour bacteria) out of the way. Get the vet to worm your pets before your baby starts to crawl and then regularly every few months.

However clean you keep the house, once your baby is crawling around she will certainly need a bath in the evening to clean off the results of the day's explorations. Bathtime can be great fun with a variety of plastic ducks and containers, a lightweight plastic jug and funnel and a watering can for discovering the fascinations of water-play.

Entertaining Your Baby

During this period your baby will still enjoy the toys mentioned in the previous chapter (pp.39-40). She will particularly appreciate toys which make a noise, such as drums, some bells or a tambourine. She will also have fun with toys which she can operate herself: a simple, not-too-noisy jack-in-the-box, a jumping man on a string, a wooden hen which clucks as you pull it along. Look for robust toys that are simple to operate.

Once your baby can sit up, she will get a great deal of pleasure from playing in a sandpit. It's not difficult to make one by filling a large, shallow, wooden or plastic box, or cheap plastic washing-up bowls or storage boxes with sand (depending on how much space you have), or by digging one in the garden, if you have one.

Make sure you get 'silver sand' from a garden or hardware shop. Supply some small light spades or big spoons and a variety of containers for filling with sand, and always cover the sandpit with a lid or piece of polythene when it's not in use to keep cats out.

It's amazing how many toys a baby of this age accumulates, and you'll need to find somewhere indoors to keep these. A practical solution is a wicker or plastic laundry basket or a shallow wooden box into which you can heap everything after use, and from which it's easy for your baby to get what she wants during the day. Alternatively, you could use cheap, oblong, plastic washing-up bowls which can be stored on open shelving later on. Whichever you use, keep the box, basket or bowls of toys in the kitchen, sitting room or wherever you are during the day, so that your baby can play close to you.

Sharing Activities

'Close to you', not to say all over you, is the operative word during this stage. You will find that you cope best if you can accept this, plan your activities with this in mind, and draw your baby into as many of them as possible.

This can be frustrating, because everything will be accomplished much more slowly and less efficiently. The key is not to set your standards too high; mentally to slow down your own pace and remember that all the time you're in fact doing two jobs – the practical task in hand, and the most important job, that of looking after your baby.

She will love to help dust the furniture and sweep the floor; to stand up at the sink on a chair and dabble her hands in the water while you're washing up; to play with some pastry trimmings when you're baking.

A trip to the shops can be the highlight of her day, especially if you talk to her about all the interesting things you pass on the way, and the goods you're putting into your trolley. Let your baby feel the bulkiness of a loaf of bread, the coldness of a packet of frozen peas, the lightness of a packet of crisps. Then when you get home, let her help you to unpack your bags and put the things away.

Make every effort to build up a feeling of the two of you as a team, coping with things together – and having fun together – rather than getting into

48

the habit of thinking of your baby as an impediment preventing you from doing what you want to do. A warm feeling of companionship created now, will grow and stand you in good stead for the future.

What with the clutter which a baby makes about the house and the demands she makes on your time, unless you have a great deal of domestic help it's impossible to maintain high standards of tidiness and housekeeping.

This is easier if you're not terribly house proud than if you're naturally inclined to worry about every mark. But you will be far happier - and so will your baby - if you can resign yourself to having just a quick tidy-up once a day than if you feel that things ought to be tidier all the time. Why? Who for? The most important thing at this stage is for your baby to be happy and for you to relax and enjoy her.

When my babies reached this stage I found that, in contrast to the early baby days, I coped best if I had some sort of routine to the day. Periods of play with bricks, sand, water, quiet times looking at picture books and playing with other toys, interspersed with walks to the shops or the park or to feed the ducks, and a blessed period in the late morning or early afternoon when the baby slept.

If you are at home all day you are quite likely to find that coping with a lively 'into everything' baby, doing the essential shopping, making an evening meal and keeping the house in some sort of rough order occupies your whole day and takes every ounce of energy, leaving you exhausted in the evening with very little to show for your labours except one happy, thriving, rosy-cheeked little person.

Going Back to Work

Much the same could be said about tiredness if you are working full-time or part-time. Here your major concern will be balancing the demands of your job with the many needs of your family and at times you will feel stretched to the limit. On top of this, you will probably feel guilty for leaving your baby. But returning to work has both positive and negative aspects, so try and accept this without regrets. As my birth counsellor, Gill Thorn, says:

'The popular image of an organised woman with her family life under control so that it never interferes with her work is a myth. The best you can hope for is that your arrangements hold up most of the time. You'll juggle work and motherhood and may feel that you are doing neither job well; your baby will probably be perfectly happy!'

Getting your support network and childcare arrangements sorted out so that you are completely happy with them is of course a priority. Helpful books and information on this are available (see Useful Addresses). You need to think about it at an early stage - while you are still pregnant is not too early - particularly if you want your baby to go to a good day nursery.

If you know in advance what sort of hours you want to work, and you think your employer would be open to such ideas, it might be worth discussing your plans in advance. Make sure that you familiarise yourself with company policy on maternity leave and maternity pay beforehand.

Clingy Babies

It is hard that the time for returning to work often coincides with a natural phase in your baby's development when they become fiercely attached to you. They can become very upset every time they lose sight of you, even if it is only for a few moments.

This phase passes quickly if you give your baby the reassurance she needs by staying with her as much as possible. She cannot understand that if you go away you will come back: she does not know enough. The more you try to stop her from clinging by going away, the more insecure and fearful she will get.

Even if you are planning to be at home full-time, it's a good idea to get your baby used to another

49

person: perhaps a relative or neighbour whom she knows well enough to be left with when you have to go away for short periods. On the other hand, it is obviously best if you can keep the times when you're away from your baby to the minimum while this 'clingy' period lasts. By giving her what she needs during this intensely emotional time you'll help it to pass as speedily as possible. You will also create an emotional security that will enable your baby to make happy and fulfilling relationships throughout her future life.

If you are planning to return to work, it is important to give your baby plenty of time to adjust to her minder, nanny or carer at the nursery. Leave your baby for an hour or so to begin with, gradually building up to a full day over a period of weeks if you can.

That way your baby will come to know her 'substitute mum' and know that you always come back. You, in turn, will feel relaxed and happy, knowing that your baby is settled. Don't expect to feel quite 'normal' when you return to work, though; remember you have been through a major experience and that you are still adjusting mentally, emotionally and physically. Just treat yourself gently and keep reminding yourself, 'I'm doing the best I can'.

Feeding Problems

Some babies are very fussy eaters which makes mothers worry, wondering how they can tell if their baby is getting enough food. If your baby is healthy, lively and growing, then you can be sure that enough food is being consumed even if it seems like too little.

Do not worry if your baby really does not like some food, because you can usually find another source of the same nutrients. It is far better to stick to foods which you know your baby likes - and avoid battles of will. And do not worry if your baby eats her food in the 'wrong' order or mixes things up. As long as she's eating nutritious foods, it really doesn't matter how she eats them.

It also helps if you can encourage your baby to feed herself from an early age. Protect her clothes with a sensible bib - the plastic ones with pockets in which to catch spilled food are good - and the floor under the highchair with newspaper, which looks messy but can be thrown away and renewed, or with plastic sheeting, which has to be wiped clean. Put the food in front of your baby and let her feed herself. This will be an undeniably messy business at first but it will be worth it in the end and with practice her competence will grow.

Sleeping

Babies need less sleep in their second six months, and if yours is a particularly lively baby you may soon find her sleeping time during the day reduced to two short periods or one longer one (if that).

Whether your baby actually sleeps or not, it's a good idea to plan your day to include two brief 'rest' times, when you settle her into her cot. Provide plenty of interesting things for her to look at or get on with quietly until she actually falls asleep. But if she doesn't go to sleep, make sure that you do not leave her to 'rest' for too long, so that she starts to become bored and unhappy.

During this period, often around nine months, many babies go through a phase of being difficult at bedtime. A baby who has hitherto gone to bed quite happily will become very clingy, screaming and crying and not wanting you to leave the room. This is really a night-time extension of the emotional clinging described on p.35.

Once again, the quickest way to get through this stage is to give your baby the comfort she needs and assure her of your physical closeness. But at the same time you have to ease yourself away, or you will find yourself trapped into having to sit with your baby until she falls asleep - which could be quite a lengthy process.

Preparing for Bedtime

Prepare for bedtime by making the hour preceding it as happy and loving as possible. Try to avoid upsets and conflicts at this time. Warn your baby that bedtime is approaching and build up a bedtime routine that you follow each day: perhaps a pleasant bath, playing with the ducks and other toys in the water, then a trip downstairs to say 'goodnight' to the rest of the family.

Then up to the bedroom for a story, a 'goodnight' kiss for the favourite toys, a kiss and a cuddle for your baby and a favourite lullaby. After this, tell your baby that she must go to sleep, that you're going downstairs but you'll pop back in a moment or two. Keep popping back and also calling out encouragingly as necessary.

If your baby really won't release you, it may be helpful if you can arrange to delay your parting by planning to tidy and put away clothes in her bedroom so that you're close while she is going off to sleep. Go out when this is done, but again, keeping popping back reassuringly often, and certainly either pop back or call out reassuringly if your baby cries out.

This way you'll build up her confidence that you're still there and that her needs will be answered, and gradually the difficult phase will pass. Whatever you do, try not to pick your baby up and bring her downstairs, even once, as this will create bad habits for the future.

You've got to be loving but firm; which isn't always easy. I think we're often afraid to be firm, but it can be done in a kind and loving way, reassuring your baby at the same time that you're still close and caring, but also that you're not going to pick her up or play.

Waking at Night
Sometimes a restless, wakeful pattern may develop during the night around this time, too. This can be extremely wearying when you're physically exhausted by the demands of a lively and increasingly mobile baby.

Often there is no apparent reason for the wakefulness, but it's worth checking the obvious things such as whether your baby is warm enough – one of those baby bags' will keep her cosy if she kicks the covers off; whether there is some noise that is waking her up and, if so whether you can improve the situation by moving her bed to a different position, putting up thicker curtains or even double-glazing; whether she is waking because of nappy rash making her bottom sore (protect her with a thick layer of cream and a one-way nappy at bedtime).

If none of these things makes any difference, it's quite tempting to think that your baby is waking herself up on purpose, just to be annoying. This of course is impossible: just think how difficult it is for adults to wake themselves up by strength of will, let alone a tiny baby. Neither can babies of this age do things for effect, either to annoy or please you. Their interest can, however, be stimulated by a response from you which amuses or interests them, so don't reward a wakeful baby by being chatty or scolding.

There may be some subtle reason for your baby's restlessness. It may be that she unconsciously feels the need for more cuddling, or is upset by something in her day's routine. Sometimes this night-time waking is associated with trying to wean a baby too quickly, for instance, when she still needs the comfort of sucking. So mentally check on these things next.

If none of these applies – or the problem is no better – there is nothing you can do but accept the situation and make the best of it. It may be helpful to find out whether it works best to leave the baby to cry for ten minutes – some give up and go back to sleep – or go in immediately. If you have the kind of baby that you have to go in to, you'll probably find it best to get up quickly, the moment she starts to cry. She will probably go back to sleep quickly as soon as she's reassured of your presence, and you too can go back to bed and, with any luck, also fall asleep again quickly.

It's worth bearing in mind that it's natural for babies (and adults) to wake several times in the night and they have to learn how to drift off again without help. If they habitually go to sleep

51

sucking a nipple or dummy they cry when they wake because they haven't learned to get back to sleep without the nipple or dummy in their mouth. This tends to happen if a baby is breastfed and then put into her cot asleep, or has a dummy to go to sleep. I'd try to put a baby to bed (for naps or at bedtime) sleepy, but not asleep, to help her learn to drift off on her own.

Waking Too Early

Some babies wake at a most unsociably early time in the morning and this too can be a problem. But it's no good expecting a baby refreshed by a night's sleep to go back to sleep again. It's better to arrange for the room to be lit with a low-power nightlight and leave some suitable toys within reach. It may even be worth making the effort to get up and give her a drink or change her nappy, if this will mean she will play happily in her cot for a while and give you a little longer in bed.

When Your Baby is Six to Eight Months Old

You will find that as your baby takes more solid food, her demand for milk will decrease. Your baby will suck from you for a shorter time and eventually give up the milk feed entirely. Your milk supply will decline correspondingly; the reverse of the process that enabled you to produce enough milk in the early days.

You will probably find it takes two or three days for your body to catch up with your baby's decreased demand, and your breasts may feel rather full, but this transition period only lasts for a few days.

You can now begin to enrich the simple fruit and vegetable purées with vegetarian protein ingredients. Any of the foods described on page 53-4 can be added.

Once your baby is taking these solids happily, you can give an enriched vegetable purée as a main course, followed by a fruit purée or yoghurt or cereal-based mixture as a 'pudding'.

You can also begin introducing solids before the other main feeds of the day, so that eventually the feeds that correspond to breakfast, lunch and supper are composed entirely of solids.

You will also find that, as your baby gets used to the texture of solid foods, there is no need to be so particular about puréeing the food. In fact it is good for her to get used to a bit of texture in food at this stage. I soon found I only needed to mash food for my babies, although I know other babies can be more fussy.

You will gradually be able to drop first one milk feed and then another, so that by the time your baby is around nine months the early morning and bedtime feeds may well be the only ones left. Do not be in a hurry to wean your baby from the bliss of these, especially if you are working during the day; it is important for the closeness to you and the emotional satisfaction the sucking gives. Some babies have spontaneously given these feeds up by the time they are one year old, but many continue well into their second year.

At this stage, particularly if your baby is teething, you can introduce some finger foods. Your baby may find it comforting to chew on something hard: a piece of apple, raw carrot, bread or rusk, but never leave a baby alone with food like this because of the danger of choking. If anything gets stuck in your baby's throat, be ready either to hook it out quickly with your finger or else turn her upside down and smack her gently in the small of the back until the object is dislodged.

Suggested Feeding Pattern, from Six to Eight Months Old:

– ON WAKING: Breast/bottle-feed
– Breakfast: Baby rice or muesli cereal or enriched fruit purée; breast/bottle-feed
– MID-MORNING: Diluted fruit juice from a spoon or cup (or give this drink mid-afternoon)
– LUNCH: 1-2 tablespoons enriched vegetable purée, or lentil purée, followed by some fruit purée for dessert (optional); breast/ bottle-feed – until your baby gives this up
– MID-AFTERNOON: Diluted fruit juice from spoon or cup (unless this was given in the morning)

52

Finger foods: slices of apple, carrot sticks, wholemeal rusk
— DINNER: Same as breakfast; breast/bottle-feed
— BEFORE BED: Breast/bottle-feed

■ VEGETARIAN PROTEIN ENRICHMENT FOODS FOR WEANING

Orange lentils
contain iron for healthy blood
Made into a thick soup, see recipe section, these make a wonderfully nutritious meal for a baby. Serve as it is, or with a little crustless wholemeal bread mashed into it; or make soup extra thick and add to a vegetable purée.

Mashed beans
contain iron and B vitamins for healthy blood and growth
Use home-cooked beans (soya beans, red kidney, cannellini, baked beans, etc), or canned ones, well rinsed, to remove salted water. (Don't use canned ones before baby is eight months old.) Mash thoroughly or purée.

Beans in tomato sauce
contain iron and B vitamins for healthy blood and growth
These make a quick and nutritious meal from eight months onward. Choose a variety without preservatives or colourings and if possible without salt or sugar. Mash or purée. Can be mixed with crumbled wholemeal bread and a little boiled water to moisten.

Tofu
for a range of nutrients which may include calcium, for healthy bones, if calcium sulphate was used in the processing
Drain tofu, mash thoroughly, then mix with vegetable or fruit purées.

Tahini, smooth peanut butter, almond, hazel, cashew, pumpkin seed butter
for a range of nutrients including iron, calcium, B vitamins and valuable oils
Mix a little - perhaps $1/2$ teaspoon at first - into vegetable or fruit purées. Choose a smooth peanut butter without salt or additives, such as emulsifiers and stabilisers. Really good health shops stock other types of nut and seed butter which are delicious.

Yeast extract
for B vitamins including B12, for healthy blood and growth
Use a low-sodium one from the healthfood shop. Add a little - $1/2$ teaspoon at first - to vegetable purées.

Nutritional Yeast Flakes
concentrated source of B vitamins for healthy growth
Use a debittered brand which you can get at good health shops, and sprinkle sparingly just a pinch - over baby's vegetable purées or breakfast muesli mix. Can also be added to a mashed-banana and yoghurt mix.

Finely milled nuts and seeds
excellent source of proteins, healthy oils, iron and other nutrients for healthy blood and growth
Powder the nuts in a blender, food processor or clean electric coffee grinder, or use ground almonds. If you're grinding your own, use a variety of nuts - almonds, hazel nuts, peanuts, walnuts, pumpkin and sunflower seeds - for a full range of nutrients. Stir into fruit or vegetable purées, starting with $1/2$ teaspoonful.

Wheatgerm
full of nutrients including iron for healthy blood and vital B vitamins for healthy growth and development
Sprinkle sparingly over fruit or vegetable purées; add to cereal mixes and yoghurt for splendid nourishment.

Cottage cheese; low fat soft white cheeses such as fromage frais, ricotta
excellent source of calcium for healthy bones
Give this from eight months, choosing one that's preservative-free, low-salt, preferably organic and, in the case of cottage cheese, not too lumpy. Mash into fruit or vegetable purées, or mix with finely shredded watercress or very finely grated carrot and cheese, a little wheatgerm, some

53

nutritional yeast flakes or yeast extract for a healthy baby salad mix. Fruit-flavoured fromage frais makes a popular and nutritious pudding but try to find one that's as natural and low in sugar as possible (and again, organic if possible).

Hard cheese
excellent source of calcium for healthy bones
Choose a hard cheese, with no colourings or preservatives, organic if possible. Grate finely; add to puréed vegetables, starting with $^1/_2$ teaspoonful.

Yoghurt
good source of calcium for healthy bones
Choose an active plain yoghurt, organic if possible. Add to fruit purées or give as it is, with a little Date Spread stirred in and a sprinkling of wheatgerm and/or powdered nuts. Mashed with banana and wheatgerm, and perhaps a little tahini, and some powdered nuts, this makes a quick baby meal.

Eggs
excellent, balanced protein and some iron
Eggs - free-range and organic if possible - always need to be thoroughly cooked to avoid the risk of salmonella. Try mashing the yolk of a hard-boiled egg into a vegetable purée. If this goes down well, try well-cooked scrambled eggs. Don't introduce egg until your baby is 18 to 24 months old if you have any history of allergies, asthma or eczema in the family.

Hummus
for excellent balanced protein, calcium and iron
Good quality bought, or homemade, can be given as it is, or mixed with bread or cooked vegetables. For excellent balanced protein, calcium and iron.

■ WHEN YOUR BABY IS EIGHT TO TWELVE MONTHS OLD

If your baby takes well to solids, you will quite soon find that she will easily and naturally eat a little of what you, as a family, are having. If you're in doubt about the suitability of certain foods, check them against the 'Cautionary Notes' in this book. The main thing to watch is that your baby's portion is not too highly seasoned or salted. Sometimes it's possible to take out a small quantity for your baby before adding spices and seasonings. For instance see instructions given for Dal Sauce on page 73.

If your baby gets used to trying new flavours, it will make it possible for you to eat out with friends or in a restaurant. Simply select a suitably unspiced or lightly seasoned dish from the menu. Check the suitability of various foods - or ask for an unsalted omelette or just vegetables (and grated cheese if you're not vegan) and mash your baby's portion with a fork.

At this stage you may need to consider the amount of fibre your baby is getting. Since a vegetarian diet is naturally high in fibre, which facilitates the passage of food through the intestines, it's important for your baby to have some concentrated sources of nourishment each day as well, such as egg, cheese, yoghurt, powdered nuts, yeast and yeast extract (unsalted), tahini, tofu and peanut butter.

If your baby's diet becomes too laxative, it can cause a very sore bottom. In this case it may be advisable to give a bread that is lower in fibre than wholemeal. Try wheatgerm bread, or, if this is still too fibrous, get an enriched white one. Try a higher fibre bread again when your baby is a little older.

At this stage, between nine months and one year, your baby will probably have an eating plan that goes something like this:

Suggested Feeding Pattern, from Eight or Nine Months On:
— *ON WAKING*: Water or diluted fruit juice from cup
— *BREAKFAST*: Muesli or porridge; wholemeal toast or bread with low-sodium yeast extract
— *MID-MORNING*: Diluted fruit juice
— *LUNCH*: Mashed nut or pulse savoury with vegetables; fruit purée and cereal pudding or fruit with yoghurt or custard; water or milk

54

— MID-AFTERNOON: Diluted fruit juice; finger foods (e.g. slices of apple, carrot sticks, wholemeal rusk)

— DINNER: Wholemeal bread with cottage cheese, nut butter or lentil spread; or scrambled egg on bread or toast, or Very Quick Lentil Soup with wholemeal bread (see page 81); carrot sticks, pieces of raw cucumber, slices of apple; fruit with yoghurt or cereal pudding as at lunch; water or milk

— BEFORE BED: Breast/bottle-feed

This second year marks the transition from babyhood to the toddler stage and great progress

55

The vegetarian toddler

is made. It's a delightful and interesting period during which your baby learns a large number of new skills and becomes even more of a companion.

In many ways a one to two-year-old is still very much a baby; yet at the same time she feels a growing awareness of her own identity and need for independence. It can therefore also be quite a turbulent time for you both, and humour and a philosophical attitude, plus plenty of patience, will help you to cope.

The secret during this period, and indeed throughout childhood, lies in being sensitive to your child's needs; being careful not to push her towards independence too quickly, yet at the same time avoiding treating her too much as a baby and so causing rebellion and aggression.

You are still the centre of your toddler's life and she is just beginning to learn that she wants to please you. Before, she was not aware of you as a person separate from her. Yet, on the other hand, she feels an increasing need for independence and may suffer an inner conflict as a result.

You can help by gently teaching her to be independent, being sensitive both to her need and her capability, helping her to cope with each stage as soon as she is ready, but without pushing her faster than she can manage to go. Praise her for being, full stop. That is, praise her for what she is, not what she does.

That way she cannot fail, and she will learn what pleases you by your attitude, not your words. Watch that you do not inadvertently put pressure on her so that she feels she has to reach an impossible standard in order to get your approval.

Children, even within the same family, are so different and I think one of the secrets of successful handling is to be able to let your child set the pace while being on the lookout for signs that she is ready to be helped to cope with a new skill.
I know this is a controversial subject, but I must say I found it very helpful with my own children

to know a little about their type of character and temperament from their horoscope. I found the information which this gave extremely valuable; in fact I wouldn't like to have to bring up a child without it.

The information is general enough to avoid moulding the child in a preconceived way but gives many helpful pointers for bringing the best out of the particular temperament which, by the age of two, it's becoming obvious that the child has. See, Useful Information for further details.

Play and Development
During this year physical skills increase dramatically and you'll need to expand the boundaries of your baby's safe play area accordingly. Try, as before, to make the area safe and baby-proof rather than have the worry of the possibility of the toddler getting into danger or mischief, or the strain of constantly having to restrict her or say 'no'. Be clear in your own mind about where you will draw the boundaries, but have as few of these as possible.

Remember, toddlers have short memories, strong emotions and live in the present; a child of this age simply does not understand the difference between 'being good' and 'being naughty', so do not expect the impossible.

Encouraging Independence
Make sure your toddler is not thwarted in her movements by clothes which are stiff, uncomfortable or too big. They should be soft and comfortable to wear so that they don't restrict vigorous play; have easy-care things which can go straight into the machine and don't need ironing

At this stage of rapid growth it's a waste of money to buy special clothes for best. Buy normal clothes which you can use for best when they're new, then for everyday wear after that. Cheap and cheerful, easy-to-do-up, washable, drip-dry clothes are the best choice from both your point of view and your toddler's, with a washable all-in-one anorak suit for cold days and wellington boots for splashing through puddles.

57

Apart from the fun of playing with sand, water and mud, a toddler can only concentrate on one thing at a time and if she is busy trying to climb up a muddy bank she won't be able to think about keeping her clothes clean.

Make the most of your child's urge for independence and help her to achieve it. Show her, for instance, how to slide safely off the bed by rolling on to her tummy and sliding off, feet first, and how to negotiate the stairs safely.

When you're showing your toddler how to do something, make a conscious effort to slow your pace right down. We take familiar actions, such as doing up a button or tying shoelaces, so much for granted, forgetting how many small actions are involved in the process.

Try doing things with the other hand from the one you naturally use to get an idea of how your toddler, with her lack of coordination, feels. Break up each process into tiny stages and teach these to your child slowly, one at a time, so she gradually learns the complete skill.

Encouraging Curiosity

Every day is full of discovery for a child of this age and it is a revelation to see something apparently boring, like a walk to the shops, through her eyes. You suddenly find yourself noticing all kinds of things such as fire engines and car-transporters, and it becomes so automatic to point these out that you may find yourself doing so to an amazed company of adults when your toddler isn't with you. Even visits to the supermarket can be fun if you let your baby take a lively interest in your shopping. Talk about the things you're buying, enlist her 'help' over what you need, which item to choose, then let her examine the things as you put them in the trolley.

As a change from the daily routine, toddlers love trips to different places: a visit to a farm-trail or zoo, a trip on a train or the top of a bus for a change from the car. These will stimulate her

interest and give plenty for her to look at and point to. You can help the development of her language by talking about the things that you see, drawing her attention to different colours and shapes. It's a good idea to carry a packet of plain (unsalted) mini rice cakes and some apple juice, water or a mixture of the two, for a healthy snack. A banana, tangerine or some seedless grapes also make good snacks as do little hummus sandwiches, small packets of raisins or dried apricots.

Encouraging Individuality

Help your toddler begin to make decisions by asking her to make simple choices (and stick to them!): 'Which sock shall we put on first?' or 'Which colour brick shall we pick up next?'

It's best to avoid presenting her with complicated choices where she hasn't the experience to know which she'd enjoy most and will worry that she's going to make, or has made, the wrong choice. To ask 'Would you like to go to the park and play on the swings or go to the pool and feed the ducks?' is probably too difficult for her; it's better to say 'Let's go to the park and play on the swings' and save the alternative for another day.

It's good experience, too, for your toddler to have the chance to play with another child of her own age. 'Playing together' at this stage usually only amounts to toddlers watching one another, and for the most part each getting on with their own activities, with you intervening fairly frequently when one pinches the other's toy. Babies become very possessive about their toys at this stage, and your efforts to take something away will be met with howls of rage. So always be quick to offer an alternative toy or activity.

Toys for Toddlers

Regarding suitable toys for this age group, your toddler will still have fun with all the toys mentioned in the previous sections. In addition they'll enjoy:
— water play and bricks, as well as sand
— cups or rings which stack into or on to each other and teach the first concept of bigger and

smaller. With these your toddler will also be able to learn the meaning of into and on to, inside and outside, through putting things into boxes and playing hide-and-seek with her toys

- toys which push and pull along - these are great fun
- a posting box, which teaches the recognition of different shapes
- simple jigsaws and tray jigsaws
- a large cardboard box which she can crawl into will give her hours of fun

Discipline and Punishment

What is discipline? Not punishment, but teaching. I, personally, am not in favour of smacking children, especially when they're as young as this. When a baby or young child looks to you for love and comfort, it seems to me to be abusing that trust suddenly to inflict physical pain on the child.

It's equally bad to discipline a young child by putting emotional pressure on her, pretending to cry if she does something naughty; giving warmth and love when she is 'good' and being cool when she is 'naughty'. A baby of this age is too young to understand the consequences of her actions, that if she pulls the tablecloth everything will fall on to the floor, if she drops your best vase it will break.

Even if she did understand these things, her memory is short and a toddler lives very much in the present. So although she may promise not to pull out your drawer of sewing things again - and mean it at the time - a few minutes afterwards she will have forgotten all about it and will undoubtedly do it again later.

To scold her for it would be confusing because she has genuinely forgotten about the last time and is too little to understand the concept of 'promise', anyway. It's better to secure the drawer or move your sewing things to a higher one and put some bricks or other toys in the one she keeps opening. This second course of action is the best because not only does it harmonise the situation, it also gives your baby the satisfaction of being able to do something positive for herself - to open 'her' drawer and get some toys out.

This demonstrates one of the secrets of handling a toddler well: avoid confrontation whenever possible and look for a positive way of dealing with a situation. If she gets something she can't have, divert her with something else that's 'much more fun'; if you want her to fetch something and she says 'no', challenge her to a race: 'I bet you can't get it before I've counted to five.' She'll get it, 'win', and have fun at the same time.

Once you get into the habit of thinking in these ways it's surprising how many potentially difficult situations can be turned into fun. This way you can make your toddler do what you want her to do.

Coping with Tantrums

If you adopt the policies described above, you will (mostly) avoid exhausting tantrums and the bond between you will grow stronger and warmer as you 'have fun' together and generally meet life's challenges as a team. However, there will almost certainly be times when you or your baby are tired and you mismanage or misjudge the situation, or when things are complicated by some other factor and a tantrum results.

Once the child is in the grip of a tantrum, she is coping with an emotional force too strong to control. She is incapable of stopping and may be frightened by the strength of her own emotions. She may shout and scream and rush around the room, crashing into everything that's in her path, or throw herself to the floor, kicking and screaming. She may even stop breathing and appear to lose consciousness briefly, though paediatricians assure us that children cannot permanently damage themselves this way.

During the Tantrum

Keep as calm as you can when dealing with this situation; try at all costs to avoid screaming back at your child even though you, too, feel at the end of your tether.

When she is in the grip of a tantrum she genuinely cannot do anything about it. Take immediate steps

59

to remove anything dangerous or breakable. It's generally best to hold your child firmly either on the floor, if that is where she has ended up, or on your lap. Then she will gradually calm down and can be cuddled and comforted.

If holding your child only makes the tantrum worse, just move anything dangerous or breakable out of the way and wait until she has calmed down before cuddling and comforting her.

After the Tantrum

Go ahead with whatever you had planned; don't alter your plans in response to the tantrum or punish the child by stopping an activity she enjoys. Let her see that you accept the tantrum as something which she cannot help.

Try not to reward her with extra (disapproving) attention after a tantrum; do not let her see that you're upset by them or worried about the possibility of her having one in an awkward place. Try not, for instance, to treat her any differently if she has a tantrum when you're visiting a very prim and proper friend than you would do if it happened at home.

I realise that's difficult, because most of us are so aware of the disapproval of others and this does change our behaviour; but that's the ideal to aim for. Continue to do your best to handle your toddler in such a way as to avoid tantrums as much as possible, but to treat them as calmly and matter-of-factly as you can when they do arise, and very soon you'll find you're through this stage.

Resting and Sleeping

This is often an in-between period for rests as your toddler makes the transition from two naps a day to one long one. You will probably find yourself constantly adjusting your timetable and the hour at which you have your lunch.

Many toddlers end up having quite a long rest in the middle of the day, then as they get older they want to go down for this later and later so that it begins to interfere with bedtime. When this

happens your toddler may have to be woken from her rest before she's really ready.

Most toddlers hate being woken up from a rest and you'll need to allow time for cuddles and comforts as you gently help your toddler to ease herself into the waking world again.

Bedtime can still be a problem for a baby of this age, with difficulty in getting her to settle down and go to sleep and begging you to stay. I do not hold with the 'leave her to cry whatever happens' philosophy; I think it's best to aim for an extension of the policy described in the previous chapter.

Follow a soothing bedtime ritual, as described on p.50-1, spend a little time tidying or pottering about, in or close to your toddler's bedroom, then say a final 'goodnight' and go. But be prepared to go straight back if your toddler starts to cry seriously (as against one or two sleepy cries).

When you go back, reassure your child that you're still there, that she hasn't been deserted. Having done this in a cheerful but firm manner, go out again. If you keep this up long enough she will get bored, yet at the same time she will finally drop off to sleep with the comforting thought that you're not far away and that you care.

Some toddlers do take an awful long time to get bored, though. So aim to do the very minimum necessary to reassure your child: you have to use trial and error to discover what this is. Trying though it is, this phase, also passes and you'll soon have forgotten all about it.

Nightmares

Sometimes during this year a toddler goes through a phase of waking up, terrified, with nightmares. When this happens, all you can do is to go to her, cuddle and reassure her until she's comforted, then settle her back to sleep.
It's worth thinking about any possible reason for these disturbances. Is she going through a

particularly stressful period, for some reason? And if so, can you think of any ways of taking the pressure off? Perhaps she is being weaned too quickly or is anxious because of overzealous potty training? Perhaps her routine has been disrupted in some way, or maybe there is a new baby in the family? Be extra loving and tolerant, take special care to keep to her familiar routine and generally 'baby' her a bit, until her sense of security returns.

Potty Training

Since a child is physiologically unable to control her bladder and bowels until 15 months at the very earliest, there's absolutely no point in starting potty training, or even buying a potty before then. The important thing with potty training is to relax – and let it happen.

Remember that babies vary a good deal in the time it takes them to get 'clean' and 'dry', and if your particular child is later than some it's no reflection on either you or her. It's not a race, and all babies get potty-trained eventually even though you may begin to wonder whether yours is going to be the great exception.

To start with, babies are totally unaware of their bodily functions. Then, suddenly one day, when your toddler is about to have a dirty nappy, she notices the physical sensation and realises that something is about to happen, though not soon enough to stop. Once this has happened, you can produce the pot and suggest that next time she might try going in that instead of in her nappy. But don't appear too eager: try and be fairly unemotional about the whole thing. You will find your toddler will get the idea.

Toddlers are able to control their bowels first; bladder control takes longer, because the sensation of passing water, especially into a nappy, isn't so noticeable. It will help your toddler to become aware of what is happening if you can let her have some periods of play without a nappy. It's a great help if this stage coincides with some warm summer weather and your toddler can run about in the garden without a nappy. Then, when she makes a puddle, she will suddenly notice what

is happening. However, don't expect too much too soon, because noticing what is happening and actually being able to control it and reach the potty in time are two different things.

You'll need plenty of patience, clean pants and damp cloths to wipe up the many puddles. But gradually your toddler will get the idea of telling you – probably by clutching herself strategically – when she's about to make a puddle, and hang on long enough for you to reach the potty or lavatory.

You can, by the way, get a special children's lavatory seat which fits over the ordinary one. Unless your toddler is frightened of the lavatory, I don't think these are worth bothering with. It's better, in my opinion, to help her to get used to coping with the ordinary lavatory as soon as possible.

Getting out of Nappies

Once you've got to this stage, I think it's best to abandon nappies in favour of towelling pants or disposable trainer pants during the day, using a nappy just at night and if you're going out and don't want the risk of a puddle.

Much as you're longing to be rid of nappies, do try not to get emotional about potty training. If you show pleasure when your toddler manages to use the potty, she has the means of displeasing you, and by this stage also the capability of using it.

If you're having problems, not showing you're either pleased or displeased can defuse the situation. Accept it calmly when your toddler uses the potty, but equally accept that there are bound to be many 'accidents' too. Try to be even-tempered about these, and certainly don't scold your toddler for them; she isn't doing it on purpose just to be annoying, and she will get dry.

Once she does, you'll find when you go out that you've simply swapped nappy-changing gear for a pot which you'll be taking everywhere with you, until she's got enough control to hang on while you find a lavatory. People who haven't had this experience can have no idea how this searching-for-public-toilets stage slows up shopping expeditions and other trips: but, again, it doesn't last long.

Even after she is reliably dry during the day your baby will probably continue to need to wear a nappy at night for quite a while. Once she can do away with this, it's useful to use a disposable bed mat which you can buy at any chemist and put on the bed in case of accidents at sleep-time, throwing it away and replacing with another if it gets soaked.

■ FEEDING YOUR VEGETARIAN TODDLER

A well-balanced vegetarian or vegan diet is perfectly safe for toddlers and young children (as indeed it is for all age groups) and your toddler will thrive on it. Occasional sensational news items headlined 'starving vegetarian babies' have always referred to babies being brought up on an extremely restricted and unbalanced diet, just of fruit or rice or some-such, not the kind of balanced and varied diet which we normally mean by 'vegetarian' or 'vegan' and as described in this book.

All the same, tiny children have specific dietary needs and it's important to see that these are met.

Energy

Babies between the ages of 6 and 12 months need 700 to 1000 calories a day. This means they need to have some concentrated sources of energy such as good quality vegetable oil – you could stir $1/2$ to one teaspoonful of an omega-balanced oil into their breakfast cereal or over other foods (but don't heat it) – avocado, cheese, ground almonds, smooth almond or peanut butter, tahini, lentils cooked with oil. Sugar supplies energy but contains no nutrients and is not a good food for babies.

Fibre

One problem with a vegetarian/vegan diet is that many of the foods, although nutritious, are also rather high in fibre, and while that is a good thing for adults, young children may not be able to chew enough to obtain all the nutrients in a concentrated form. So watch out for this and base their meals on some of the less-fibrous foods, including plenty of the ones mentioned above. Fresh fruit and vegetable juices are an excellent source of vitamins and minerals; just give a little, diluted half-and-half with water.

Never give a baby refined bran; if a baby seems constipated, give plenty of water or fruit juice to drink. Prune juice over breakfast cereal, in yoghurt or diluted with water is good, too.

Protein

Many people worry about getting enough protein in a vegetarian diet. But as long as you include some concentrated sources of protein at each meal, your baby will be getting plenty. If you're worried, remember milk or soya milk to drink, and milk or soya milk puddings like fromage frais, yoghurt, soya pudding are excellent ways of boosting protein.

Iron

Iron is another nutrient you need to keep your eye on. Babies are born with a store of iron but this is used up by the time they are six months old. Good sources of iron for a baby from six months include:
– puréed dried apricots
– prune juice
– molasses
– split red lentils
– puréed or well-mashed beans (red kidney, etc)
– green vegetables (again, mash or purée as necessary)
– cereals, but don't give very bulky, fibrous cereals for reasons described above and also because bran can inhibit a baby's ability to absorb some minerals, including iron.

Calcium

Milk, whether breast-milk or formula will supply your baby with all the necessary calcium in the early days. Once solids are introduced and gradually become the main source of nourishment you need to make sure to include good sources of calcium. These include:

- full fat cow's milk or soya formula milk (see note on p.15)
- cheese
- sesame seeds and tahini (sesame cream)
- ground almonds
- tofu
- beans and lentils
- green vegetables
- wholemeal bread.

Vitamin D

Vitamin D is found in cheese, milk, eggs and yoghurt, also in fortified foods such as some breakfast cereals and margarine. It is also formed by the action of sunlight on the skin. It may be difficult to get sufficient, particularly if your baby is vegan so a vitamin D supplement, in the form of drops, is a sensible precaution: ask your doctor.

Vitamin B12

Vegetarian babies will get sufficient B12 from dairy products. For vegan babies, foods which have been fortified with B12, such as some soya milk, veggieburgers or low-sodium yeast extract need to be a regular part of the diet.

Food Cautions

The following are foods which need to be given with care, or avoided.

Salt and Sugar

Salt can put too much of a strain on a baby's kidneys. Don't add salt to food you cook for your baby and avoid salty foods such as chips and savoury snacks, salted stock, soy sauce and yeast extract (except for low sodium). Sugar supplies calories without nutrients and encourages a sweet tooth and tooth decay. Your baby will discover it sooner or later, but the later the better. Don't give sweet squash or fizzy drinks and always dilute pure fruit juice with water.

Spices

As with salt, spices such as curry powder, pepper, nutmeg and mustard can stress a baby's kidneys so it's best not to introduce them too early.

Refined flour and flour products

Unless you specifically go for organic varieties, these will probably contain additives such as bleaching agents, preservatives and so on, and may also contain traces of chemicals used in the growing process (fertilisers, pesticides) which can cause allergies. But 100% wholemeal flour and bread may be too high in fibre for some babies under 12 months.

Honey

Although raw organic honey has been found to have some healing properties, honey is not recommended for young babies because it is such a concentrated form of sweetening and also because of the risk of food poisoning. Honey can be introduced to your child from 1 year.

Processed foods with additives

Not recommended at any age, but especially not for babies because of the danger of allergic reactions. Some additives have been linked with hyperactivity and aggression in young children. Permissible ones, in my opinion, include canned beans, baked beans (low salt, low sugar) and tomatoes – in all cases choose organic brands if possible.

Nuts

Whole or chopped nuts are unsuitable for children under five years because they can get stuck in their throat and cause choking. They can be used in their finely ground or 'butter' form and are a useful and nutritious food. However some experts recommend delaying their introduction because of the risk of allergies developing. If you have a history of allergies in your family it's best not to introduce nuts until your baby is at least three years old and to avoid eating them when pregnant or breastfeeding.

Quorn and TVP

The manufacturers of Quorn do not recommend it for children under two; and textured vegetable protein (TVP) tends to be rather salty and difficult for small children to digest.

63

Caffeine

Found in coffee, tea, cola drinks, chocolate and products made from cocoa, caffeine is a stimulant and not suitable for young children.

Alcohol

Because of their small body weight, the undesirable effects of alcohol are magnified if it is given to young children. Also in countries where is normal to give young children diluted wine, this is being linked with alcoholism later in life.

Deep-fried foods

Whilst some fat is desirable, too much isn't good, and heating certain types of oil to the temperatures required for deep frying alters the chemical structure, making it potentially harmful.

Skimmed/semi-skimmed milk and soya milk

A baby needs the extra fat and calories in whole milk. Skimmed, semi-skimmed and soya milk are too low on these. Use whole milk until your child is five years old (semi-skimmed after two years in certain cases, under medical supervision) and soya formula milk ideally until the age of five. If you do use normal soya milk between two and five years, do make sure that the lower energy content is compensated for by other foods as part of a well-balanced diet.

Eggs

Organic free-range eggs are a good food for vegetarian babies over the age of six months (though some experts recommend avoiding them until a baby is 12 months). Do ensure that the eggs are always thoroughly cooked to avoid the risk of salmonella. Boiled eggs, in particular, always need to be cooked until both the yolk and white are solid, approximately 8-10 minutes.

■ ONE WEEK'S MENUS FOR YOUR TODDLER'S LUNCH AND DINNER
(Dishes marked * are suitable for freezing)

LUNCH	DINNER
Tofu Potato Cakes with Parsley Sauce* and carrot sticks. Segments of orange. Milk or soya milk.	Wholemeal bread with peanut butter or Tahini Dip and slices of tomato. Grated apple with yoghurt, raisins and wheatgerm. Milk or soya milk.
Leftover pasta in tomato sauce with grated cheese, nutritional yeast flakes or ground almonds. Finely grated apple with a little yoghurt and wheatgerm. Milk or soya milk.	Hummus* with fingers of wholemeal toast. Carrot sticks. Millet and Raisin Cream. Milk or soya milk.
Baked potato mashed with a little finely grated cheese or tofu and finely grated carrot. Banana mashed with a little yoghurt and grated pumpkin seeds. Milk or soya milk.	Very Quick Lentil Soup* and wholemeal roll. Raw broccoli florets. Ripe pear slices. Milk or soya milk.
Leftover Lentil Soup with wholemeal bread mashed into it. Slices of tomato. Fresh fruit prepared for finger-feeding. Milk or soya milk.	Hummus* with broccoli florets, carrot sticks and wholemeal toast. Slices of apple. Milk or soya milk.
Leftover Lentil and Broccoli Gratin,* reheated and mashed with skinned tomato. Soaked dried apricots puréed with yoghurt, topped with sprinkling of wheatgerm.	Spicy Beanburger* with watercress and carrot sticks. Muesli: yoghurt mixed with rolled oats, wheatgerm, finely grated apple, raisins, powdered pumpkin seeds. Milk or soya milk.
Scrambled egg or Scrambled Tofu on crumbled wholemeal bread with shredded watercress. Segments of orange.	Red Kidney Bean and Avocado Salad with shredded lettuce and carrot sticks. Fingers of wholemeal bread with yeast extract. Slices of apple.

64

■ LUNCHES YOU CAN SHARE WITH YOUR BABY OR TODDLER
(Dishes marked * are suitable for freezing)

YOUR LUNCH	BABY'S LUNCH	NOTES
Baked potato with grated cheese or mashed cooked beans. Lettuce, tomato and grated carrot. Banana with yoghurt and wheatgerm.	The inside of a baked potato, mashed with a little milk, grated cheese or puréed cooked beans. Banana mashed with a little yoghurt and wheatgerm. Milk.	Your baby can have a little very finely grated carrot and mashed skinned tomato mixed with the potato too.
Baked beans on wholemeal toast. Watercress. Sliced peach with yoghurt, wheatgerm and chopped nuts.	Baked beans mashed with crumbled wholemeal bread (soak in a little water if necessary to make bread mashable) Skinned peach mashed into yoghurt, sprinkled with wheatgerm. Milk.	Choose a brand of baked beans that does not have preservatives or colourings and preferably one that has reduced sugar and salt.
Very Quick Lentil Soup* with wholemeal roll. Tomato and watercress. Fresh fruit.	Very Quick Lentil Soup with wholemeal bread mashed into it. Fresh fruit pieces prepared for finger-feeding. Milk.	Freeze leftover soup in usable portions for future use.
Cheese or Tahini Dip sandwiches. Tomatoes, lettuce and carrot sticks. Fresh fruit.	Wholemeal bread mashed in a little warm milk or soya milk with grated cheese or Tahini Dip. Fresh fruit, mashed, grated or prepared for finger-feeding. Milk.	See page 71 for Tahini Dip recipe.
Avocado filled with cottage cheese or Tahini Dip and shredded spring onion, with lettuce, tomato and watercress. Fresh fruit.	Avocado mashed with cottage cheese or Tahini Dip and very finely shredded watercress. Fresh fruit, mashed, grated or prepared for finger-feeding. Milk.	Choose a small, ripe avocado.
Hummus* with pitta bread and sprigs of raw cauliflower and carrot sticks.	Hummus with wholemeal bread mashed into it. Sprigs of cauliflower and carrot sticks for finger-feeding. Yoghurt puréed with raisins. Milk.	Make or buy a hummus without much garlic. Soak the raisins in hot water or apple juice for 45 minutes or so beforehand.
Leftover Lentil and Broccoli Gratin*. Lettuce and tomato. Soaked dried apricots with yoghurt.	Leftover Lentil and Broccoli Gratin reheated and mashed with skinned tomato. Soaked dried apricots puréed with yoghurt, topped with wheatgerm.	Buy unsulphured dried apricots and soak overnight. See page 81-2 for recipe.
Red Kidney Bean and Avocado Salad on lettuce with tomato and grated carrot. Wholemeal bread. Apple, raw, or baked with filling of dates and wheatgerm, topped with yoghurt.	Red kidney beans mashed with finely chopped lettuce and finely grated carrot. Fingers of wholemeal bread or toast and yeast extract. Finger-food slices of raw apple, or finely grated apple, or mashed baked apple and date with yoghurt. Milk.	Canned beans (without colouring) are fine from eight months on. Put beans into a sieve and rinse under cold water to remove some of the brine.
Scrambled egg or Scrambled Tofu on wholemeal toast. Watercress. Orange.	Scrambled egg or tofu on crumbled wholemeal toast. Skinned orange segments for finger-feeding. Milk.	Remember to cook the egg thoroughly, to avoid the risk of salmonella. See page 97-8 for recipe.

65

■ SUGGESTIONS FOR BABY'S AND TODDLER'S LUNCHES

When you're preparing a midday meal for a baby or toddler, it's very convenient to be able to make something you can eat too. And it's got to be quick and easy! There are plenty of simple, delicious dishes that you can enjoy for lunch and share with your baby, either as they are or by adapting them slightly (suggestions for labour-saving shared meals on p.65).

While babies will usually eat what they're given, often with great relish, when they get to the toddler stage (between 15 months and four years old) and develop minds of their own, feeding can become more of a problem. They often have passionate likes and dislikes, and I've met many mothers who are worried that their toddler hardly seems to be eating enough to keep a sparrow alive.

I've been through this stage with my own children, so I know the kind of inner panic that can easily set in as yet another meal is barely touched. Paediatricians say reassuringly that no child of this age will starve in the face of food, so if your child is obviously thriving, in spite of minuscule meals, then you do not have to worry too much. The most important thing is for you to remain calm and not allow a tense atmosphere to build up at mealtimes.

Putting it into Practice

To sum up, the following foods provide an excellent daily nutritional basis for your toddler:
- 600ml/1 pint whole milk or soya milk formula or equivalent in cheese or yoghurt
- 25g/1oz vitamin-enriched breakfast cereal, or the equivalent described below
- two thick slices wholemeal bread
- 75ml/3 fl oz orange juice or 75-100g/3-4oz orange
- Vitamin D and, if necessary, B12 supplement

To these you need to add, in particular, foods that are rich in iron. Children of this age can be extremely fussy, and some foods will be more readily accepted than others, so choose wisely. Some suggestions would be 1-2 daily servings of pulses, peanut butter, finely ground almonds or pumpkin seeds; a serving of potato or grain such as brown rice, millet, wholemeal pasta or wholemeal bread (in addition to the above); dried fruit (including prune juice if liked); yeast extract; wheatgerm; and as many raw and cooked vegetables (including a daily serving of leafy vegetables if possible) as your child will eat.

Here's how this scheme works out in terms of meals:

Menu Plans for the Vegetarian/Vegan Toddler:

- *BREAKFAST*: Fortified wholemeal cereal with milk or soya milk, a sprinkling of wheatgerm, nutritional yeast flakes and raisins; wholemeal toast with yeast extract; milk. Or rolled oats, flaked millet, and wheatgerm soaked in prune juice with chopped dates and grated Brazil nuts; milk. Or chopped banana, wheatgerm, grated Brazil nuts, chopped dates, yoghurt; wholemeal toast with yeast extract; milk. Or cereal or oat mix as above; boiled egg with fingers of wholemeal bread or toast; milk
- *MID-MORNING AND/OR MID-AFTERNOON*: Orange juice diluted with a little water (or prune juice, if your toddler is getting enough vitamin C from other sources, see p.14)
- *LUNCH AND DINNER*: (see p.65)
- *BEDTIME*: Milk

In planning the menus for one week's lunch and dinner menus for your toddler, I have allowed a pulse dish either at lunch or dinner; a green vegetable either at lunch or dinner; bread, pasta, cereal or potato at either or both; a fruit and milk pudding or its equivalent. Make sure that your toddler is getting 600ml/1 pint whole milk or soya milk formula during the day.

Eating Between Meals: Healthy Snacks

Snacks between meals are not necessarily a bad thing if they're nutritious. Indeed, they may be the most acceptable and harmonious way of getting nourishment into a difficult toddler! Here are some ideas for between-meal nibbles that

66

contribute positively to the diet:

— Carrot sticks
— Celery sticks filled with cottage cheese, Hummus or Tahini Dip
— Fingers of wholemeal toast (or whole wheat rusks) with peanut butter, hummus or tahini dip
— Figs, dates, raisins and dried apricots
— Whole almonds, Brazil nuts and pumpkin seeds (given under supervision, in case of choking, from around five years old)
— Molasses Flapjacks (see page 112 for recipe)
— Yoghurt-and-fruit milk shakes
— Homemade yoghurt or orange juice ice lollies
— Nutty Carob Bananas (see page 114 for recipe) Healthy Ice Cream
— Cubes of cheese
— Brown rice cakes (with no added salt) from the healthfood shop

■ SURVIVAL TIPS

— Do not worry if your child really does not like some food; you can usually find another source of the same nutrients. It's better to stick to foods you know will go down well - and avoid battles of will.
— Paediatricians say reassuringly that no child of this age will starve in the face of food, so if your child is obviously thriving, in spite of minuscule meals, then you do not have to worry too much. The most important thing is for you to remain calm and not allow a tense atmosphere to build up at mealtimes.

— All children go through a stage when they learn the power of the word no. If this veto is used over food, you may be able to nip it in the bud by offering a choice of two equally nutritious items instead of single suggestions they can refuse.
— Do not worry if your toddler eats foods in the 'wrong' order or mixes things up (after all, that's part of the fun, spoilsport!); and don't set too high a standard.
— If there's a problem over food, the secret is not to get emotional about it, either because you're worried about your toddler's health or because it's hurtful to have your food refused. It simply isn't worth making an issue over food or allowing a difficult situation to develop. In fact, as always, it's your relationship with your child that's the most important thing. This is what you're building up and what will endure long after you've forgotten the horrors of broken nights, tantrums, food fads, and puddles on the carpet! Always put this relationship first, before a spotless house, before rigid timetables, before battles over food or anything else, and you will be rewarded by the deepening bond of understanding and companionship that will develop between you, and last a lifetime.

67

PART 2

RECIPES

In this section you will find a selection of favourite recipes to help you to put into practice the suggestions in the first half of the book. They are mainly quite quick and easy to make, and appeal to a wide range of age groups. Where applicable I've added notes on what to serve with them, whether they're suitable for a baby or toddler and any adaptations that need to be made. Many of them freeze well and I've added notes on that, too. I hope you will enjoy them.

EASY DIPS AND DRESSING

VINAIGRETTE

If you're making a bowl of salad, and everyone likes dressing, it's easiest to mix it straight into the bowl, but if you want to add vinaigrette individually it can be handy to have some made up in a jar ready for use. Vary the proportions of oil and vinegar according to your own taste. Balsamic vinegar gives a sweet, mellow flavour; I've recently taken to using organic apple cider vinegar for its health-giving properties.

Put 1 teaspoon of sea salt into a jar with a grinding of black pepper, 2 tablespoons of vinegar, 6 tablespoons of olive oil and shake well.

Children can have a little vinaigrette on salads from about a year old, but remember not to make it too salty.

DATE SPREAD

This is useful for sweetening yoghurt and other puddings; also for spreading on bread and butter or toast. Simply chop 100g/4oz cheapest dried dates (not sugar-rolled) roughly, removing any stones or hard pieces. Put the dates into a small pan with 150ml/5 fl oz of water and heat gently for 5-10 minutes, until soft. Beat to a purée with a wooden spoon and allow to cool. This keeps for at least a fortnight in a jar in the fridge.

SESAME SALT – GOMASIO

This Japanese seasoning, which is used instead of salt, is a useful way of eating calcium-rich sesame seeds and reducing salt. Sprinkle it over savoury dishes, steamed vegetables, grains, salads and use as a dip for crudités. Put 10-12 teaspoons sesame seeds into a dry pan with 1 teaspoon sea salt. Stir over a moderate heat for 1-2 minutes until the seeds pop, smell roasted and brown a little. If you're making this for babies or toddlers, just leave out the salt.

YOGHURT DIP OR DRESSING

Simply mix chopped fresh herbs into unsweetened natural yoghurt – soya or dairy – along with salt, pepper and some crushed garlic to taste. Peeled, diced cucumber can also be added. Herbs, which are especially good, are mint, coriander, flat leaf parsley or chives.

TAHINI DIP OR DRESSING

Tahini dip makes an excellent topping for salads or filling for sandwiches. Packed with protein, iron, calcium and B vitamins, it's particularly valuable for increasing your milk supply when you're breast-feeding (see page 35) – but it's good any time, for adults, babies and children. You can make it thick, as a dressing or dip, to have with raw vegetables or strips of wholemeal pitta bread; or thin, as a creamy, pouring sauce, which is good with steamed vegetables.

To make enough for one, put 2 tablespoons of pale tahini into a small bowl with a crushed garlic clove (or less, to taste) and the lemon juice and stir. The mixture will go very thick and lumpy; add a little cold water and continue to stir. It will gradually become smooth and creamy. Go on adding water until it's the consistency you want, then season with salt and pepper – or leave out the seasoning if you're making it for a baby or toddler.

HUMMUS

Although you can buy good hummus, it's easy to make your own, and worth it if you eat a lot of it. To make enough for two adults, drain a 425g can of chickpeas, reserving the liquid. Put them into a food processor with 1-2 crushed or grated garlic cloves, 2 tablespoons pale tahini, a tablespoon of lemon juice and 4 tablespoons of the reserved liquid. Whiz until smooth. Add more liquid if you want a thinner mixture. Season as required. Hummus is great with salad, as a dip with raw vegetables or bread, or as a filling in sandwiches. Children love it once they get the taste for it, and it's extremely nourishing. You can introduce hummus to your children from the age of 6 months onwards but go easy on the garlic if giving it to a baby.

CHEESE DIP

Children adore this. Serve it with pieces of raw carrot, celery, cucumber, cauliflower... if you're making it for young children, you might like to leave out the spices and pepper. Put 40g/1^{1}/2 oz softened butter into a small bowl and beat with a wooden spoon until softened. Mix in 150g/5oz finely grated Cheddar cheese, a little at a time, followed by 6 tablespoons of milk, also bit by bit, so you end up with a creamy consistency. Season as required with salt, pepper, a dash of tabasco, and a little grated nutmeg.

EASY BEAN DIP

Babies can have this from 6-8 months.
Drain a can of cannellini beans, keeping the liquid, then whiz or mash with a squeeze of lemon juice and some finely chopped chives or parsley. Add enough of the reserved liquid to make a creamy consistency. Serve with fingers of wholemeal toast or pieces of raw vegetable.

QUICK AVOCADO DIP

Delicious for grownups and a good food for babies from about 6-8 months but best without the cheese until the baby is over 8 months - and go easy on the tabasco!

Halve a ripe avocado and remove the stone. Put into a bowl with a tablespoonful of lemon juice and mash a fork, season as required with salt, pepper and a dash of tabasco sauce. Chopped tomato, fresh coriander and curd or ricotta cheese can be mixed in with the avocado.

TOFU AND HERB DIP

Babies can have this from 8 months.
Put a drained block of tofu into a food processor with a small handful of parsley, a small garlic clove, crushed, 2 tablespoons of lemon juice and some salt and pepper, as required. Whiz to a smooth cream. This is lovely spread on crispbreads or rice cakes.

Quick sauces

A quickly made sauce can turn a few cooked vegetables or some pasta into a meal. Here are four easy ones, three of them rich in protein. For more on pasta, see p.106-10

EASY TOMATO SAUCE

Although you can buy jars of tomato sauce, many of them have all kinds of unwanted additives like extra sugar, modified starch and salt. But it's easy to make your own, and it freezes well. Fry a chopped onion in 1 tablespoonful of olive oil for 10 minutes, until soft. Add a crushed or chopped garlic clove, a 425g/15oz can of chopped tomatoes and simmer, uncovered for 15-20 minutes, until the mixture looks thick. Serve as it is, or purée in a blender. Season to taste with salt and pepper required. This sauce freezes well: pour into a suitable lidded container, allowing room for the sauce to expand as it freezes (this sauce can be frozen for at least 6-8 weeks).

72

CHEESE SAUCE

Pour over lightly cooked vegetables to make a nutritious dish for children. Serve as it is, or sprinkle with more grated cheese after you've added the vegetables and brown under the grill. Any leftover sauce will freeze well for another time. Put 50g/2oz butter or pure vegetable margarine into a saucepan with 50g/2oz unbleached white flour, 600ml/1-pint milk or soya milk and a bay leaf and whisk together over a moderate heat until thickened Leave to simmer gently for 10 minutes, to cook the flour, then remove from the heat, stir in 50-125g/2-4oz grated cheese and season to taste. Remove the bay leaf before serving. For a vegan version, omit the cheese and stir in 1-2 tablespoons of nutritional yeast flakes (or to taste) instead To freeze, pour into a suitable lidded container, allowing room for the sauce to expand as it freezes (this sauce can be frozen for at least 6-8 weeks).

You can vary this sauce: to make parsley sauce, omit the cheese and stir in two good heaped tablespoons of chopped parsley. Or for spinach sauce, add a little block of frozen chopped spinach, stir and heat until it's melted and heated. You can buy packs of tiny blocks of frozen spinach and this sauce is a good way of getting some green vegetables into reluctant children.

PEANUT SAUCE

Quick to make and full of nourishment. Serve poured over any cooked or salad vegetables, or over cubes of lightly fried tofu. You can buy mirin, a naturally sweet seasoning from Japan, from good health shops. Just put 2 big rounded tablespoons of smooth peanut butter into a saucepan with 2 crushed garlic cloves, 1 tablespoon Tamari or Kikkoman soy sauce, a tablespoon of mirin (or 1/2teaspoon sugar), a tablespoon of rice or cider vinegar and 150ml/5fl oz water. Heat gently, stirring until smooth, then add 25g/1oz creamed coconut, cut into small pieces.

DAL SAUCE

Loved by children and adults alike, this is a fast and healthy way of turning a few vegetables into a meal. The spices are put in at the end so you can take out a child's portion before adding them. To make enough for four, put the a large chopped onion, 4 chopped garlic cloves and 2250g/9oz lentils into a saucepan with 1 litre/1³/4pints of water and a couple of slices of fresh ginger. Bring to the boil, then half cover and leave to simmer for 20-25 minutes, or until the lentils are very tender. At this point you can remove the ginger and purée the mixture in a blender if you want it smooth and unseasoned for a baby or toddler, or continue as follows. In another, small saucepan, stir 1 teaspoon each of turmeric, ground cumin and coriander until they smell roasted, then stir them into the lentil mixture, along with the juice of half a lemon and salt and pepper to taste.

ONION GRAVY

Fry a chopped onion in 2 tablespoons of olive oil for 10 minutes, until tender and beginning to brown. Add 2 tablespoons wholemeal flour and cook over the heat for a few minutes, until the flour is nut-brown, stirring often. Pour in 400ml/15fl oz water and add a teaspoonful of low-sodium vegetable stock, a teaspoon of yeast extract and 1-2 teaspoons tamari or soy sauce Leave to simmer over a low heat for 10 minutes, to cook the flour. Serve as it is or blend to a purée if preferred. You can increase the nutrients in this by stirring in 1-2 tablespoons of soya flour and/or 1-2 tablespoons of nutritional yeast flakes before you liquidise the mixture. They give a pleasant flavour and an almost creamy consistency. Add more water as necessary. Serve with Easy Lentil Roast on page 84, or with vegetarian sausages or burgers and mashed potatoes.

73

SIMPLE SALADS

QUICK GREEN SALAD

A fresh green salad goes with so many dishes and is an excellent way of getting your daily green vegetables. Just tear the leaves and mix them with a little Vinaigrette (p.71), any fresh herbs that you have, and any other ingredients you fancy, such as spring onion, capers or sliced avocado.

TOMATO SALAD

A tomato salad works best if you slice the tomatoes (which needn't be peeled) 30-60 minutes beforehand. Put them into a shallow dish and drizzle a little vinaigrette over them. Tear some basil over, if you have some, or add some thinly sliced onion.

MIXED ITALIAN SALAD

Make a base of torn green salad leaves; top with sliced tomato, cucumber, celery or whatever is available, and some coarsely grated carrot. Spoon a little vinaigrette over the top.

COLESLAW

Ready-made coleslaw is very over-sweet and high in fat, but it's easy to make your own that's not. Quickly shred some cabbage - I prefer to use green-tinged cabbage like Primo or Sweetheart rather than bullet-hard white cabbage. Mix with a few spoonfuls of plain yoghurt - dairy or vegan - a little vegetarian or vegan mayonnaise and seasoning to taste. You can add other ingredients such as grated carrot, chopped spring onions, raisins, chopped dried apricots, red pepper, fresh sweetcorn scraped from the cob.

CARROT SALAD

Grate some carrots then mix with fresh orange or lemon juice, seasoning to taste and any other ingredients you fancy: chopped apple, cucumber or celery, raisins, chopped herbs. Children usually love this salad; some may prefer the carrot very finely grated so that it's almost pulpy.

BEAN AND LENTIL SALADS

Drain a can of beans or lentils into a sieve and rinse under the cold tap to remove as much salt as you can (or buy unsalted ones). Put the beans or lentils into a bowl and mix with a spoonful of olive oil, a squeeze of lemon juice or a few drops of vinegar (to taste), some chopped chives, parsley, spring onions or other herbs, salt and pepper as desired. Other ingredients can be added: chopped apple, raisins, grated carrot, red pepper and for older children, chopped cashews, roasted peanuts, brazil nuts or walnuts. Red bean and avocado salad works particularly well.

GRAIN SALADS

Cooked rice, barley, quinoa, millet and buckwheat all make the basis for pleasant and filling salads. For Rice Salad with toasted seeds, mix cooked brown rice with chopped spring onion, red pepper, dried apricots, raisins, parsley and a handful of mixed pumpkin and sunflower seeds which you have toasted for a few seconds under the grill, until they're golden and smell aromatic. Add a few drops of cider vinegar and a dash of olive oil with salt and pepper; mix. You can vary the ingredients forever, and do try using some of the more unusual yet nutritious grains such as millet and quinoa.

WALDORF SALAD

Always popular with the children I know, this is just diced apple and celery mixed together with some plain yoghurt and mayonnaise and seasoning to taste, along with walnuts if the children are old enough. Raisins or seedless grapes are also nice in it, if the kids like them.

GREEK SALAD

Mix together cubes of peeled cucumber, chopped tomatoes and slices of feta cheese sprinkled with a little dried oregano. Dress with a tablespoonful of olive oil and a squeeze of lemon juice or a splash of wine or cider vinegar. Add black olives to taste and a little chopped mild onion (or spring onion) if you like.

CRUDITÉS

Just pieces of raw vegetable which kids often prefer to more complicated salads. Whole spring onions; chunky batons of cucumber, scraped carrot; celery; thick pieces of red, green or yellow pepper; cherry tomatoes or wedges of tomato; sugar snap peas or baby sweetcorn; florets of cauliflower or broccoli.

SANDWICHES AND SNACKS

FILLED PITTA BREADS

Warm pitta breads (preferably wholemeal) under the grill or in a toaster. Split in half and fill with all kinds of goodies: chopped tomato, cucumber, red pepper; coleslaw, Greek salad, p.76; drained and rinsed canned beans or lentils; grated carrot; felafel, bought or made from a packet mix and packed into pitta with shredded lettuce, tomato and hummus or tahini dressing, p.71-2; beansprouts; cubes of avocado.

BURGER IN A BUN

Cook bought veggieburgers, bean burgers or home-made bean burgers under the grill, along with a wholemeal roll for each person. Serve the burgers in the rolls with shredded lettuce and tomato, mayonnaise, healthy tomato ketchup... whatever you like. Tempeh, a fermented soya product, like a lumpy-looking brown version of tofu, is excellent sliced, fried in a little oil, sprinkled with soy sauce and served in a burger bun.

REFRIED RED BEANS IN TACOS

Mexican tacos, which you can buy at some supermarkets, will keep in the cupboard and then in the freezer once opened. Warm one through under the grill, then top with hot or cold Refried Red Beans, p.82-3, shredded lettuce, sliced tomato and some sliced or mashed avocado, and roll up firmly.

SANDWICH IDEAS

- Yeast extract, tahini, peanut butter or ricotta cheese with lettuce, bean sprouts, tomato, cress, cucumber or grated carrot

- Home-made cheese spread, or grated cheese mixed with yoghurt, soft white cheese or mayonnaise, with lettuce, tomato or cress

- Finely chopped hardboiled egg, mixed with yoghurt, mayonnaise or soft white cheese, on its own or with cress

- Scrambled egg and cress

- Home-made Tofu spread, or chopped tofu mashed into vegan mayonnaise, with cress

- Hummus, on its own or with chopped black olives and coriander

- Peanut butter, fried tempeh (see Burger in a Bun, above), tomato, spring onion or grated carrot

- Drained and mashed cannellini beans, watercress, cress, grated carrot or avocado

- Soft white cheese with chopped dates

- Tahini mixed with honey

- Mashed banana with finely grated nuts or ground almonds

- Peanut butter with finely grated carrot

- Cream cheese with canned-in-juice pineapple, drained and mashed

- Thinly-sliced cucumber with mashed Brie cheese

- Grated or thinly-sliced cheese and pickle

WHOLEMEAL GARLIC TOASTS

These are nice for serving with lentil soup. Cut fairly thick slices of wholemeal bread, toast on both sides, then brush rub a peeled garlic clove over the top of the bread and brush with olive oil. Serve at once, or pop under the grill for a few seconds to make the oil sizzle.

ROLLED SANDWICHES

Sometimes a change of presentation can make all the difference to the appeal of familiar foods. Children love these rolled sandwiches. Spread white, brown or wholemeal bread thinly with butter and cut off the crusts. Spread the bread with a little yeast extract if liked and then put a little of your chosen filling - chopped hardboiled egg, say, or grated cheese or, my favourite when I was a child, skinned and chopped tomato - in a strip on the bread about 1 cm from one edge. Then fold the edge over the filling and go on rolling the bread over, like a Swiss roll, until it is completely rolled.

You can also create a 'pin wheel' effect by spreading the bread completely with a filling which isn't too bulky, like Marmite, peanut butter or cream cheese and chopped chives, rolling as described, then cutting with a sharp knife to make slices about 6mm/^{1}/4in.

TOASTED CHEESE

Toast a piece of bread on one side. Sprinkle the untoasted side with grated cheese (dairy or vegan) and put under a hot grill until melted and golden brown. Eat as it is, or cut into pieces and serve on top of a salad. Or you can make two pieces of toasted cheese as described then sandwich them together when the cheese has melted.

MELBA TOAST

This thin, crisp toast goes well with many dips and is a healthy, fat-free alternative to crisps. Children love it. Toast sliced bread on both sides then with a sharp knife cut through the bread to split each piece in half, making each into two thin pieces. (This is easier to do if you use bread from a sliced loaf.) Cut the pieces diagonally into triangles and again into smaller triangles if you like. Place the sliced pieces, untoasted side up, on a grill pan and grill until crisp and browned - the edges will curl up. This only takes a minute or two. Cool on a wire rack. The melba toast keeps well for a few days in a tin.

WRAPS OR QUESADILLAS

Heat a flour tortilla in a dry frying pan for a few seconds on each side, to warm it through. Sprinkle grated cheese (dairy or vegan) over one half and fold the other half over. Continue to heat in the frying pan until the cheese has melted and both sides are golden. Serve at once. You can use pitta bread in the same way, stuffing grated cheese (or mashed cooked red kidney beans or even baked beans) inside the pocket.

79

BEANS AND LENTILS

VERY QUICK LENTIL SOUP

This nourishing iron-rich soup can be frozen in small portions, without the cumin, for babies and toddlers. This recipe can also be used as a dal, alongside rice and cooked vegetables. You can spice it up (for adults and older children) with more cumin and a little coriander, maybe a dash of ground cinnamon.

Serves 4

225G/8OZ SPLIT RED LENTILS

1-2 ONIONS PEELED AND ROUGHLY SLICED

2 GARLIC CLOVES, PEELED AND CHOPPED

JUICE OF ½ LEMON

SALT AND FRESHLY GROUND BLACK PEPPER

OLIVE OIL

1 TEASPOON GROUND CUMIN (OPTIONAL)

Put the lentils, one of the onions and the garlic into a large saucepan with 1 litre/1¾ pints water.

Bring to the boil, and then let it simmer for about 30 minutes, until the lentils are very tender and pale. Or cook it in a pressure-cooker on high for 5 minutes.

Stir well to get a smooth texture. Then add some lemon juice (start with 1 tablespoon), season as required and serve.

PREP TIME: 15 MIN

COOKING TIME: 30 MINS (or 5 minutes in a pressure cooker)

RECOMMENDED AGE OF CHILD: FROM 6 MONTHS

FREEZE TIME: 8-10 WEEKS

LENTIL AND BROCCOLI GRATIN

Based on one of my earliest and most popular recipes from Not Just a Load of Old Lentils, this is a good way of eating green vegetables, freezes well, and only needs a little salad - or a baked potato - to accompany it.

Serves 4

175G/6OZ RED SPLIT LENTILS

4 TABLESPOONS OLIVE OIL

1 LARGE ONION, PEELED AND CHOPPED

2.3 CM/1 INCH PIECE OF FRESH GINGER, PEELED AND GRATED

350G/12OZ BROCCOLI, WASHED, TRIMMED, DIVIDED INTO FLORETS

JUICE AND GRATED RIND OF 1 LEMON

SALT AND FRESHLY GROUND BLACK PEPPER

SOFT BREADCRUMBS

GRATED CHEESE (OPTIONAL)

Put the lentils into a saucepan with 600ml/1 pint water, bring to the boil, and then let them simmer for 20-30 minutes, until they are soft and pale.

Heat half the oil in another pan, add the onion and ginger and cook for 10 minutes, uncovered, so that it browns a bit, stirring from time to time.

Steam the broccoli until it is just tender, then put it in the base of a shallow gratin dish.
Put the lentils into a food processor or liquidizer, with the onion mixture and the lemon, and whiz to a smooth purée. It should be the consistency of double cream; add some water or milk if it is too thick. Season.

Pour the lentil purée evenly over the broccoli. Sprinkle the breadcrumbs and remaining oil on

81

top, or the crumbs and cheese (if you use the cheese, you won't need the extra oil).

Put under a moderate grill for about 20 minutes, until the top is brown and the inside piping hot. Alternatively, bake at 190°C/375°F/Gas Mark 5 for 30-40 minutes.

PREP TIME: 30 MINS

COOKING TIME: 30-40 MINS

RECOMMENDED AGE OF CHILD: FROM 8 MONTHS

FREEZE TIME: 8-10 WEEKS

SPICY BEANBURGERS

Although you can buy some good beanburgers now, they're easy to make yourself. They freeze well and can be cooked from frozen.

Serves 8

OLIVE OIL

1 ONION, PEELED AND CHOPPED

1 CARROT, FINELY CHOPPED OR GRATED

1/2 GREEN PEPPER, DE-SEEDED AND CHOPPED

1 GARLIC CLOVE, PEELED AND CRUSHED

HOT CHILLI POWDER TO TASTE (OPTIONAL)

1 TEASPOON GROUND CORIANDER

2 X 425G/15OZ CANS RED KIDNEY BEANS

50G/2OZ SOFT WHOLEMEAL BREADCRUMBS

SALT AND FRESHLY GROUND BLACK PEPPER

100G/4 OZ DRIED WHOLEMEAL CRUMBS

Set the oven to 200°C/400°F/Gas Mark 6.

Heat 1 tablespoon oil in a large saucepan; add the onion and stir. Cover and leave to cook over a moderate heat for 5 minutes, stirring occasionally.

Add the carrot, pepper and garlic and cook for a further 5 minutes.

Stir in the spices, starting with 1/4 teaspoonful of chilli powder if you're using it and cook for 1-2 minutes, then remove from the heat.

Mash the beans and add to the onion mixture, together with the breadcrumbs and seasoning to taste. Mash the mixture together very well at this stage because this is what holds it together.

Divide into eight; form into burgers and coat with the dried crumbs.

Place on an oiled baking sheet and bake until brown and crisp on one side, then turn over to cook the other side. Drain on kitchen paper and serve hot or warm.

PREP TIME: 30 MINS

COOKING TIME: 10 MINS

RECOMMENDED AGE OF CHILD: FROM 1 YEAR (BUT DON'T MAKE IT TOO SPICY!)

FREEZE TIME: 8-10 WEEKS

REFRIED RED BEANS

These are good with a salad, some tortilla chips and sliced avocado; or as a filling for tacos. Sometimes I spice the flavour up with a bit of chilli powder; add this when the onion is done and cook for a few seconds before starting to add the beans.

Serves 4

1 ONION, PEELED AND CHOPPED

1 GARLIC CLOVE, PEELED AND CRUSHED

2 TABLESPOONS OLIVE OIL

2 X 425G/15OZ CANS RED KIDNEY BEANS, DRAINED AND LIQUID RESERVED

SALT AND FRESHLY GROUND BLACK PEPPER

A LITTLE GRATED CHEDDAR OR VEGAN CHEESE

Fry the onion and garlic in the oil in a fairly large saucepan for 10 minutes, until it is soft and lightly browned.

Add the beans to the pan a few at a time, mashing them as you do so. Continue in this way until all the beans have been used, adding a little of the reserved liquid if the mixture gets too dry.

Put the mixture into a shallow dish; cover the top with grated cheese and pop under the grill until it's golden brown and bubbly.

PREP TIME: 20 MINS

COOKING TIME: 10 MINS

RECOMMENDED AGE OF CHILD: FROM 10-12 MONTHS (but don't make it too spicy)

FREEZE TIME: 8-10 WEEKS

QUICK CHILLI

Serves 2

2 TABLESPOONS OLIVE OIL

1 ONION, CHOPPED

1 SMALL RED OR GREEN PEPPER, CHOPPED

1 CARROT, GRATED OR FINELY CHOPPED

1 GARLIC CLOVE, CRUSHED

425G/15OZ CAN RED KIDNEY BEANS, DRAINED

400G/13OZ CAN CHOPPED TOMATOES

CHILLI POWDER TO TASTE

SALT AND FRESHLY GROUND BLACK PEPPER

Heat the oil in a saucepan and stir in the onion, garlic, pepper and carrot. Cover and cook gently for 10 minutes, stirring occasionally, until the vegetables have softened a bit.

Stir in the kidney beans and tomatoes, and bring to the boil. Simmer gently for about 10 minutes, until it's lost its liquid appearance and the vegetables are tender.

Stir in chilli powder, salt and pepper to taste, cook for a minute or two longer to cook the chilli powder, then serve.

PREP TIME: 20 MINS

COOKING TIME: 25 MINS

RECOMMENDED AGE OF CHILD: FROM 1 YEAR (but don't make it too spicy).

FREEZE TIME: 8 WEEKS

BORLOTTI BEANS IN COCONUT MILK

Use canned borlotti beans for this; drain them in a sieve and rinse under water to remove as much salt as possible.

Serves 4

2 TABLESPOONS VEGETABLE OIL

1 ONION, FINELY CHOPPED

2 X 425G/15OZ CAN BORLOTTI BEANS

400G/13OZ CANNED CHOPPED TOMATOES

400G/13OZ CAN OF COCONUT MILK

1 TEASPOONS TURMERIC

PINCH OF CHILLI POWDER

SALT AND FRESHLY GROUND BLACK PEPPER

A LITTLE CHOPPED FRESH CORIANDER

Heat the oil in a saucepan; put in the onion and cook gently for 10 minutes. Add the beans, mashing them a bit, then stir in the tomatoes, coconut, turmeric and chilli powder.

Simmer for 5-10 minutes, until well heated through then season to taste and serve, sprinkled with chopped coriander.

PREP TIME: 15 MINS

COOKING TIME: 20 MINS

RECOMMENDED AGE OF CHILD: FROM 1 YEAR

FREEZE TIME: UNSUITABLE FOR FREEZING

EASY LENTIL ROAST

Simple this may be, and rather bland, but children love it, hot or cold. It also freezes well before or after cooking and is very nutritious.

Serves 6-8

500G/20 OZ SPLIT RED LENTILS

2 BAY LEAVES

6 TABLESPOONS OLIVE OIL

4 LARGE ONIONS, PEELED AND CHOPPED

4-6 GARLIC CLOVES, CHOPPED

GRATED RIND AND JUICE OF 1 LEMON

SALT AND PEPPER

WHOLEMEAL FLOUR FOR DUSTING

EXTRA OIL FOR BAKING

Preheat the oven to 200°C/400°F/Gas Mark 6.

Put the lentils and bay leaves into a (preferably non-stick) saucepan, add 600ml/1pint of water and bring to the boil. Cover and cook over a low heat for 15-20 minutes, until the lentils are tender, pale gold and dry, with no water left.

Meanwhile heat 2 tablespoons of the oil in another saucepan, put in the onion and cook gently, covered, for 10-15 minutes, until the onion is tender. Stir in the garlic and cook for a minute or two more.

Mix the lentils with the onions, lemon rind and juice, mashing the lentils together as you do so. Then add salt and pepper as necessary: for adults, this needs plenty, but don't add it if babies or toddlers are going to eat it.

Form the lentils into a loaf shape and roll it lightly in wholemeal flour. Put the remaining 4 tablespoons of oil into a roasting tin and pop into the oven for a minute or two to heat.

Put the lentil loaf into the tin of hot oil, turning it so that it all gets coated (or spoon the oil over the top). Bake for about 45 minutes, until golden.

Serve with green vegetables and Vegetarian Gravy. Some apple sauce is nice with it: you could bake a couple of cooking apples (skin pierced to prevent bursting) in the oven at the same time, then simply scoop out the soft, fluffy insides, add a little sugar to taste and serve with the roast.

PREP TIME: 30 MINS
COOKING TIME: 45 MINS
RECOMMENDED AGE OF CHILD: FROM 8 MONTHS
FREEZE TIME: 8-10 WEEKS

LENTIL SHEPHERD'S PIE

If you're making this for babies or toddlers, drain the canned lentils into a sieve then rinse under the cold tap to remove as much as salt as you can.

Serves 4-6

1 ONION, PEELED AND CHOPPED

1 CARROT, FINELY CHOPPED OR GRATED

1 STICK OF CELERY, FINELY CHOPPED

1 GARLIC CLOVE, CHOPPED

1 TEASPOON DRIED MIXED HERBS

2 TABLESPOONS OLIVE OIL

425G/15OZ CAN CHOPPED TOMATOES

2 X 425G CANS GREEN LENTILS, DRAINED

SALT AND FRESHLY GROUND BLACK PEPPER

700G/1 1/2LB MASHED POTATO

25G/1OZ GRATED CHEDDAR OR VEGAN CHEESE

Preheat the oven to 200°C/400°F/Gas Mark 6.

Fry the onion, carrot, celery, garlic and mixed herbs in the oil in a large saucepan for 10-15 minutes, until the vegetables are tender.

Add the tomatoes, drained lentils and season as required.

Spoon the lentil mixture into a shallow casserole dish, spread the mashed potato on top, draw the prongs of a fork over the top to give a rough texture and scatter with the cheese.

PREP TIME: 30 MINS
COOKING TIME: BAKE FOR 45 MINS
RECOMMENDED AGE OF CHILD: FROM 8 MONTHS
FREEZE TIME: 8-10 WEEKS

VEGETARIAN MINESTRONE SOUP

Serves 4

3 MEDIUM ONIONS, CHOPPED

1 LARGE POTATO, PEELED AND DICED

1 LARGE CARROT, DICED

2 STICKS OF CELERY, SLICED

A FEW LEAVES OF CABBAGE, SHREDDED

2 TABLESPOONS OLIVE OIL

2 GARLIC CLOVES, CHOPPED

425G/15OZ CAN CHOPPED TOMATOES

2 TEASPOONS LOW SODIUM VEGETABLE STOCK POWDER

2 X 400G/14OZ CANS CANNELLINI BEANS, DRAINED AND RINSED

50G/2OZ MACARONI OR SMALL SOUP PASTA SHAPES

SALT AND PEPPER

Fry the vegetables in the oil for 10 minutes, until softening, then add the garlic and cook for a minute or two longer.

Add the tomatoes, vegetable stock powder, cannellini beans and 850ml/1½ pints of water. Bring to the boil, then simmer for 30 minutes.

Ten minutes before you want to serve the soup, add the macaroni or small pasta shapes. Cook for a further 10 minutes, then season and serve.

PREP TIME: 20 MINS
COOKING TIME: 30 MINS
RECOMMENDED AGE OF CHILD: FROM 8 MONTHS
FREEZE TIME: 8-10 WEEKS

85

GRAINS

PORRIDGE

Possibly the healthiest breakfast of all, so warming and filling, and it's really no trouble to make.

Serves 2

Put oats, preferably the lovely organic ones, into a measuring cup to come up to the 50 ml/mark - or use half a large mug - and tip into a pan. Add 300 ml/10 fl oz milk or soya milk and water mixed.

Stir over a moderate heat for about 2 minutes, until thickened. If the porridge is too thick, add more water, stirring well.

Serve topped with more milk or soya milk, a light sprinkling of rapadura sugar, no-sugar preserves, a drizzle of clear honey, grated nuts, chopped dried fruit, sliced banana...

PREP TIME: 5 MINS
COOKING TIME: 5 MINS
RECOMMENDED AGE OF CHILD: FROM 6 MONTHS
FREEZE TIME: NOT APPLICABLE

TOASTED MUESLI MIX

If you like home-made muesli, it can save time to make up a bulk supply - and if you make your own, you can use the best quality ingredients and make it to your own taste. Here's a popular mix which you can vary to taste. Agave syrup is a natural sweetener you can get from good health shops. It has a low glycaemic index so it won't raise blood sugar. It's well worth looking out for.

350G/12 OZ ORGANIC ROLLED OATS

25-50G/1-2 OZ SUNFLOWER SEEDS

25-50G/1-2 OZ PUMPKIN SEEDS

25-50G/1-2 OZ SESAME SEEDS

2 TABLESPOONS OLIVE OIL

2 TABLESPOONS CLEAR HONEY, REAL MAPLE SYRUP OR AGAVE SYRUP

2 TEASPOONS REAL VANILLA EXTRACT

Preheat the oven to 180°C /350°F/Gas Mark 4.

Put the organic oats and all the seeds into a bowl. Warm the oil and honey, maple syrup or agave syrup in a pan to ensure that it all blends together, then pour over the dry ingredients, along with the vanilla, and mix well.

Spread the oat mixture out on a large baking sheet and put into the oven. Bake for about 15-20 minutes, stirring often, until it's golden and toasted and smelling glorious, but be careful not to let it get too brown.

Cool then store in a tin.

You can add dried fruit - raisins, chopped dates and dried apricots etc to the mix once it has cooled. If you're making this for children over 5 years, you can add some of their favourite nuts, lightly chopped. Mix them in with the seeds before toasting. Serve with milk or soya milk and any chopped fresh fruit you fancy.

PREP TIME: 5 MINS
COOKING TIME: 20 MINS
RECOMMENDED AGE OF CHILD: FROM 2 YEARS UNLESS MIXTURE IS PULVERISED IN A BLENDER, THEN FROM 10 MONTHS AS LONG AS YOU DON'T USE HONEY
FREEZE TIME: NOT APPLICABLE

BIRCHER — OR FRESH FRUIT — MUESLI

This is the original muesli invented by Dr Bircher-Benner for the patients in his famous natural health clinic in Zurich. He used condensed milk because that was the only kind that was safe when he was practising at the end of the last century. You can replace this with ordinary milk, soya milk or plain dairy or soya yoghurt and a dash of honey or maple syrup to sweeten if you like, though the condensed milk gives a pleasant, almost jellied texture.

Serves 1

2 TABLESPOONS ROLLED OATS

1 TABLESPOON SWEETENED CONDENSED MILK

3 TABLESPOON COLD WATER

1 TABLESPOON LEMON JUICE

A LITTLE GRATED LEMON RIND

100 G/4 OZ GRATED APPLE OR 200 G/7 OZ SOFT FRUIT IN SEASON

1 TABLESPOONS GRATED HAZELNUTS

Put the oats, condensed milk, water, lemon juice and lemon rind into a bowl and mix to a creamy consistency. Leave overnight if possible.

Next morning add the fruit. According to Dr Bircher-Benner, the whole apple should be used, skin, core and pips!

Spoon the mixture into a serving bowl, sprinkle with the grated nuts and serve.

PREP TIME: 10 MINS PLUS OPTIONAL OVERNIGHT STANDING TIME
COOKING TIME: 0
RECOMMENDED AGE OF CHILD: FROM 1 YEAR
FREEZE TIME: NOT APPLICABLE

POLENTA

This is another dish that children like and it makes a base for adding other nutritious ingredients such as chopped parsley, grated cheese (or vegan cheese). It freezes well. You can serve it in steaming bowlfuls with a topping of cheese or a chunky tomato sauce - Easy Tomato Sauce, page 72 - or spread it out on a plate, leave it to cool and set, then serve it in pieces. You can also brush the pieces with olive oil and grill until crisp, for a change. You can buy instant polenta at supermarkets but I prefer to take the time to cook the coarser, more traditional one because it's more natural and tastier. You can buy this type from good health shops.

350G/12 OZ COARSE-GROUND YELLOW CORNMEAL (POLENTA)

2 LITRES/3^1/$_2$ PINTS WATER

SALT

BUTTER OR OLIVE OIL

GRATED CHEESE TO SERVE

Put the polenta into a deep pan - the kind you would use for cooking pasta. Gradually stir in the water and about a tablespoonful of salt - or to taste.

Put the pan over the heat and stir until it starts to simmer. Let it simmer away gently for about 40 minutes, stirring from time to time - until it's thick and all graininess has gone.

Either ladle into bowls and top as suggested, or stir in other ingredients like grated cheese or chopped parsley. Or spread it out on a plate and leave to cool and set; then warm and eat, or brush with olive oil and grill until crisp.

Plain polenta is also good with maple syrup, clear honey or a sprinkling of rapadura sugar as a pudding.

PREP TIME: 5 MINUTES PLUS OCCASIONAL STIRRING
COOKING TIME: 45 MINS
RECOMMENDED AGE OF CHILD: FROM 8 MONTHS
FREEZE TIME: 8-10 WEEKS

RICE WITH CELERY AND CHICK PEAS

2 TABLESPOONS OLIVE OIL

1 LARGE ONION, CHOPPED

4-6 CELERY STICKS, SLICED

1 RED PEPPER, DE-SEEDED AND CHOPPED

2 GARLIC CLOVES, SLICED

2 TOMATOES, CHOPPED

425G/15OZ CAN CHICKPEAS, DRAINED AND RINSED

225G/8OZ SHORT-GRAIN BROWN RICE, PREFERABLY ITALIAN ORGANIC

2 TABLESPOONS CHOPPED FRESH PARSLEY

SALT AND PEPPER

Heat the oil in a saucepan then put in the onion and celery; cover and cook gently for 10 minutes, until the vegetables are beginning to soften.

Stir in the red pepper, garlic, tomatoes, chickpeas and rice, then add 600ml/1 pint of water. Bring to the boil, cover and leave to cook gently for 40-45 minutes, until all the liquid has been absorbed and the rice is tender. Add the parsley and salt and pepper to taste, stirring them in gently with a fork.

PREP TIME: 20 MINS
COOKING TIME: 45 MINS
RECOMMENDED AGE OF CHILD: FROM 8 MONTHS
FREEZE TIME: 8-10 WEEKS

BARLEY RISOTTO

Barley can be made into a lovely risotto. The nicest type to use is organic pearl barley, which you can get from good health shops, though ordinary pearl barley is fine, too.

Serves 3-4

15G DRIED PORCINI MUSHROOMS

1 TEASPOON MARIGOLD BOUILLON

1 ONION, FINELY CHOPPED

2 STICKS CELERY, FINELY CHOPPED

2 TABLESPOONS OLIVE OIL

4 GARLIC CLOVES, CHOPPED

500G/1 LB CHESTNUT MUSHROOMS, SLICED

350G/12 OZ ORGANIC PEARL BARLEY

GLASS OF VEGETARIAN VERMOUTH

SALT AND FRESHLY GROUND BLACK PEPPER

OPTIONAL EXTRAS: 50G/2OZ BUTTER

TO SERVE: GRATED OR FLAKED PARMESAN-STYLE CHEESE, OR NUTRITIONAL YEAST FLAKES

Put the dried porcini into a saucepan with 2 pints of water and the marigold bouillon. Bring to the boil, then keep it hot over a very gentle heat.

Fry the onion and celery in the oil for 5 minutes, then stir in the garlic and chestnut mushrooms. Cook for about 10 minutes until the mushrooms have softened, then stir in the barley.

Pour in the vegetarian vermouth and when it has sizzled away, stir in a ladleful of the porcini water. When that has boiled away, add another ladleful and keep on in this way until all the water, and the porcini mushrooms in it, have been added and the barley is soft and creamy. This will take about 30 minutes.

Add the butter, if you're using this, season with salt and pepper, then cover and leave for 10 minutes. Serve with grated Parmesan-style cheese or vegan, or with nutritional yeast flakes, which have a cheesy flavour.

PREP TIME: 30 MINS
COOKING TIME: 40 MINS
RECOMMENDED AGE OF CHILD: FROM 1 YEAR
FREEZE TIME: 8-10 WEEKS

MILLET LAYER

This is a homely way of using this nutritious grain, originally based on one of Leah Leneman's recipes.

Serves 3-4

225G/8OZ MILLET

3 TABLESPOONS OLIVE OIL

2 ONIONS, CHOPPED

2 CARROTS, COARSELY GRATED

$^1/_2$ SWEETHEART CABBAGE, QUITE FINELY SHREDDED

SALT AND WHITE PEPPER

1 HEAPED TABLESPOON WHOLEMEAL FLOUR

1 TABLESPOON TAMARI OR SOY SAUCE

HANDFUL OF BREADCRUMBS

Preheat the oven to 200°C/400°F/Gas Mark 6. Put the kettle on.

Put the millet into a dry saucepan and stir it around over the heat until the grains start to pop and smell glorious. Standing back pour in 1$^1/_2$ pints boiling water - it will seethe and bubble furiously at first. Cover and leave to cook for 20 minutes.

Heat another tablespoon of oil in another pan; put in the onion, carrot and cabbage. Stir until all the vegetables glisten with the oil, then put a lid on the pan, turn the heat down and leave to cook gently until the vegetables are tender, about 15 minutes. Add salt and pepper to taste.

Heat the remaining 2 tablespoons of oil in another pan. Stir in the flour, cook for a moment or two, then pour in 300ml/$^1/_2$ pint of water. Bring to the boil, stirring. Simmer for 4-5 minutes; add tamari or soy sauce and season with salt and pepper.

Season the cooked millet with salt and pepper, then put half of it into a casserole or lightly oiled

litre/2lb loaf tin. Cover it with half of the vegetable mixture, then pour over half the sauce. Repeat the layers and sprinkle the top with crumbs.

PREP TIME: 40 MINS

COOKING TIME: 20-25 MINS

RECOMMENDED AGE OF CHILD: FROM 1 YEAR

FREEZE TIME: 8-10 WEEKS

QUINOA PILAFF WITH SUNDRIED TOMATOES, RAISINS AND PINENUTS

1 ONION, PEELED AND CHOPPED

1 TABLESPOON OLIVE OIL

2 GARLIC CLOVES, CHOPPED

225G/8OZ QUINOA

1 TEASPOON LOW-SALT STOCK POWDER

1 HEAPED TABLESPOON CHOPPED SUN-DRIED TOMATOES

50G/2OZ PLUMP RAISINS - PLUMP UP BY SOAKING IN BOILING WATER FOR A FEW MINUTES IF NECESSARY

HANDFUL OF BLACK OLIVES, OPTIONAL

HANDFUL OF TOASTED PINENUTS, OPTIONAL

SALT AND FRESHLY GROUND BLACK PEPPER

600ML/1 PINT OF WATER

Fry the onion in the oil in a large saucepan, with a lid on the pan, for 10 minutes. Stir in the garlic and cook for a minute or two longer.

Put the quinoa in a sieve and rinse under the cold tap, then add the quinoa to the onion along with the stock powder and 600ml/1 pint of water.

Bring to the boil, cover and leave to cook gently for 20 minutes. Then remove from the heat, put a clean cloth over the pan and leave to stand for 5 minutes.

Add the sundried tomatoes and raisins, the olives and pinenuts if you're using them, and serve.

PREP TIME: 15 MINS
COOKING TIME: 20 MINS; PLUS 5 MINS STANDING TIME
RECOMMENDED AGE OF CHILD: FROM 1 YEAR (but very finely chop or omit the nuts)
FREEZE TIME: UNSUITABLE FOR FREEZING

EGYPTIAN RICE AND LENTILS

This classic Middle Eastern dish is packed with protein. I love it with lots of onions added, but if your children don't take kindly to them you can always reduce the quantity.

Serves 4

2 ONIONS, PEELED AND SLICED

4 TEASPOONS OLIVE OIL

3 GARLIC CLOVES, CHOPPED

2 TEASPOONS CUMIN SEEDS

350G/12 OZ BASMATI RICE

400G/16 OZ CAN CONTINENTAL LENTILS, DRAINED

SALT AND FRESHLY GROUND BLACK PEPPER

3-4 TABLESPOONS CHOPPED FRESH CORIANDER, OPTIONAL GARNISH

Fry the onions in the oil, in a pan with a lid, for 10 minutes, until they are soft, then add the garlic and cumin and fry, uncovered, for a further 10-15 minutes, until very soft, golden and caramelised.

Heat the lentils in their liquid in a saucepan. When they're heated through – about 5 minutes – drain and gently mix with the rice and half of the onions.

Season with salt and pepper. Top with the remaining onions and chopped coriander if using.

PREP TIME: 10 MINS
COOKING TIME: 30 MINS
RECOMMENDED AGE OF CHILD: FROM 9 MONTHS
FREEZE TIME: 8-10 WEEKS

TOFU SATAY WITH RICE

A way of serving tofu that is really delicious. You need to allow 2 hours for the tofu to soak up the marinade but the recipe itself is very easy. Serve with boiled rice and an Oriental-style salad or steamed carrots (cut diagonally into oval slices) or mangetouts.

Serves 2

275G/10OZ PACKET FIRM TOFU, DRAINED AND CUBED

3 GARLIC CLOVES, PEELED

2 TABLESPOONS SOY SAUCE, TAMARI OR KIKKOMAN

2 TABLESPOONS VEGETARIAN MIRIN OR VEGETARIAN SWEET SHERRY

1 TABLESPOON RICE VINEGAR OR WHITE VINEGAR

125G/4OZ BROWN OR WHITE BASMATI RICE

2 SLIGHTLY ROUNDED TABLESPOONS SMOOTH PEANUT BUTTER

25G/1OZ CREAMED COCONUT

SALT

Put the tofu on a shallow plate. Crush 1 clove of garlic, mix together with the soy sauce, vegetarian sherry and vinegar, and pour over the tofu. Stir gently, then leave for at least 2 hours. Heat the oven to 200°C/400°F/Gas Mark 6.

Drain the tofu, reserving the marinade. Put the tofu on a baking tray in a single layer and roast in the top of the oven for 25-30 minutes, until it is well browned and fairly crisp.

Meanwhile cook the rice in plenty of boiling water – as you would pasta – until a grain feels tender when you bite it. This will be in about 9-10 minutes for white Basmati rice, 15-20 for the brown type. Drain and keep warm.

Make the satay sauce. Crush the 2 remaining cloves of garlic and put into a small saucepan with the peanut butter, the reserved marinade and 150ml/5 fl oz water. Heat gently, stirring, until smooth. Cut the creamed coconut into small pieces and stir into the sauce. Season with salt and serve out onto plates with the rice and tofu.

PREP TIME: 15 MINS (PREP) AND 2 HOURS MARINATING

COOKING TIME: 30 MINS

RECOMMENDED AGE OF CHILD: FROM 1 YEAR

FREEZE TIME: UNSUITABLE FOR FREEZING

TOFU AND STIR-FRIED VEGETABLES

A quick main course which is packed with B vitamins.

Serves 2

225G/8OZ MUSHROOMS

1/2 AN ONION OR 3-4 SPRING ONIONS

225G/8OZ BROCCOLI OR MANGETOUTS, BABY SWEETCORN OR ANY OTHER SUITABLE VEGETABLE

GROUNDNUT OIL

275G/10OZ BLOCK OF FIRM TOFU, DRAINED

2.5CM/1 INCH PIECE FRESH GINGER, GRATED

1 GARLIC CLOVE, PEELED AND CRUSHED

1 TEASPOON CORNFLOUR

1 TABLESPOON SOY SAUCE

1 TABLESPOON VEGETARIAN SHERRY

50G/2OZ CASHEW NUTS (OPTIONAL)

SALT AND FRESHLY GROUND BLACK PEPPER

Wash and slice the mushrooms; chop the onions and broccoli; top and tail the mangetouts if using.

Fill a medium saucepan one-third full with groundnut oil and heat. Meanwhile, cut the tofu into cubes and blot them on kitchen paper. When the oil is hot enough to form bubbles around a chopstick, drop in the tofu, in one layer. Deep-fry, drain on kitchen paper and keep warm. You may need to do them in two batches.

Heat 2 tablespoons oil in a large saucepan or wok. When it's smoking hot put in all the vegetables, the ginger and garlic, and stir-fry for 2-3 minutes until everything is heated through and beginning to get tender but still quite crunchy.

Combine the cornflour with the soy sauce and sherry and pour in. Stir for 1-2 minutes until thickened, then add the tofu, and the cashew nuts if using. Stir gently for 1 minute, season with salt and pepper, and serve with boiled rice.

PREP AND COOKING TIME: 30 MINS

RECOMMENDED AGE OF CHILD: this dish can be given to children FROM 1 YEAR onwards but is really more to the taste of adults than children

FREEZE TIME: UNSUITABLE FOR FREEZING

MICROWAVE RISOTTO

It's blissfully easy to make a creamy risotto in the microwave. The American cookery writer, Barbara Kafka, developed this method. You can add other ingredients to vary this recipe; some frozen petit pois are nice to add before you microwave it for the last time.

Serves 2-3

25G/1OZ BUTTER

2 TABLESPOONS OLIVE OIL

1 ONION, PEELED AND CHOPPED

3 GARLIC CLOVES, PEELED AND CRUSHED

125G/4OZ BUTTON MUSHROOMS, SLICED

175G/6OZ ARBORIO RICE

50G/2OZ FRESH PARMESAN-STYLE CHEESE

SALT AND FRESHLY GROUND BLACK PEPPER

750 ML/1¼ PINTS BOILING WATER

A LITTLE PARED LEMON RIND, OPTIONAL

Put the butter and oil into a deep, non-metallic ovenproof casserole. (At every stage, keep the casserole uncovered and microwave on high.) Put into the microwave and microwave for 2 minutes.

Add the onion and garlic and mushrooms and stir to coat in the butter and oil. Microwave for 4 minutes.

Add the rice, stir, then microwave for 4 minutes.

Pour in 750ml/1 pints boiling water. Microwave for 9 minutes.

Stir well, then microwave for 9 minutes more.

Remove from the oven. Leave the risotto to stand uncovered for 5 minutes, to let the rice absorb the rest of the liquid, stirring several times.

Flake the Parmesan style cheese with a potato peeler or sharp knife, then stir this in, together with salt and pepper to taste, scatter with a few strands of pared lemon rind if liked, and serve.

PREP AND COOKING TIME: 40 MINS
RECOMMENDED AGE OF CHILD: FROM 1 YEAR
FREEZE TIME: UNSUITABLE FOR FREEZING

BUCKWHEAT PILAFF WITH PEAS

Buy the untoasted type of buckwheat from a health shop – it's easy to toast it yourself and has a better flavour. This pilaff is good served hot, warm or cold, as a salad.

Serves 2

125G/4OZ BUCKWHEAT

1 TABLESPOON OLIVE OIL

300ML/½PINT WATER

½TEASPOON VEGETABLE STOCK POWDER

125G/4OZ FROZEN PETIT POIS

2-3 SPRING ONIONS, CHOPPED

2-3 TABLESPOONS CHOPPED PARSLEY OR MINT

SALT AND PEPPER

Rinse the buckwheat in a sieve under cold water. Shake it dry.

Heat the oil in a saucepan, put in the buckwheat and stir over the heat for about 5 minutes, or until the buckwheat turns golden brown and smells gorgeous.

Pour in the water and add the stock powder. Bring to the boil, then cover, reduce the heat and leave to cook gently for 12-15 minutes, until the water has been absorbed and the buckwheat is tender.

Stir the peas (thaw them quickly if necessary by putting them into a sieve and pouring boiling water over them), spring onion and herbs into the buckwheat; season and serve.

PREP AND COOKING TIME: 30 MINS
RECOMMENDED AGE OF CHILD: FROM 8 MONTHS
FREEZE TIME: UNSUITABLE FOR FREEZING

93

CHEESE AND EGGS

CHEESE FRITTERS

These are very popular with all the children I've known. They do take a bit of trouble to make, but can be done in stages. They freeze beautifully and can be fried from frozen. I find it worth making a double quantity and freezing half.

Serves 4

600 ML/1 PINT MILK OR SOYA MILK

1 SMALL ONION, PEELED AND STUCK WITH 3-4 CLOVES

1 BAY LEAF

150 G/5 OZ SEMOLINA

125 G/4 OZ GRATED CHEESE

1/2 TEASPOON DRY MUSTARD

SALT AND FRESHLY GROUND BLACK PEPPER

1 LARGE EGG, BEATEN WITH 1 TABLESPOON WATER

DRIED CRUMBS

OIL FOR SHALLOW FRYING

SLICES OF LEMON, SPRIGS OF PARSLEY

Put the milk, onion and bay leaf into a saucepan and bring the milk to the boil.

Remove from the heat, cover and leave for 10-15 minutes, for the flavours to infuse.

Take out and discard the onion and bayleaf. Bring the milk back to the boil, then sprinkle the semolina over the top, stirring all the time.

Simmer for about 5 minutes, to cook the semolina, then remove from the heat and beat in the cheese, mustard and some seasoning.

Spread the mixture out to a depth of about 1 cm/1/2 inch on an oiled plate or baking tray. Smooth the top. Cool completely.

Cut into pieces; dip each first in beaten egg and

then in dried crumbs. Shallow-fry in hot oil until crisp on both sides, drain well on kitchen towels. Serve at once, garnished with lemon slices and parsley sprigs.

PREP TIME: 1 HOUR

COOKING TIME: 30 MINS

RECOMMENDED AGE OF CHILD: FROM 1 YEAR

FREEZE TIME: 8-10 WEEKS

CHEESE AND ONION ROLL

This was my favourite dish when I was a little girl. It's easy to make, so don't let the thought of the pastry put you off.

Serves 4

3 LARGE ONIONS, PEELED AND CHOPPED

225G/8OZ PLAIN WHOLEMEAL FLOUR

2 TEASPOONS BAKING POWDER

125G/4OZ BUTTER

125G/4OZ GRATED CHEDDAR CHEESE

Preheat the oven to 200°C/400°F/Gas Mark 6. Put the onions into a saucepan with 1cm/1/2in of water, bring to the boil and simmer for about 10 minutes, until tender. Drain well in a colander. (The water makes excellent stock.)

Sift the flour and baking powder into a bowl or food processor; add the butter and whiz, if you're using a food processor, or mix in with a fork or with your fingers until the mixture looks like coarse breadcrumbs. Add 3 tablespoons of cold water and whiz again briefly or press with your fingers to make a ball of dough.

Put the dough on a lightly floured board and pat into a rough rectangle, and then roll it out quite thickly into a rectangle. Don't worry if it breaks a bit.

95

Lift the pastry onto a baking sheet. Spread the onions on one half of the pastry then put the cheese on top of the onions. Fold the uncovered piece of pastry over on top of the cheese and onions and press the edges to keep all the filling in. Prick the top.

Bake for 25-30 minutes, until the pastry is set and crisp.

Vegan Version

Use vegan margarine to make the pastry and grated vegan cheese or 4 tablespoons of nutritional yeast flakes instead of the grated cheese.

PREP TIME: 45 MINS
COOKING TIME: 30 MINS
RECOMMENDED AGE OF CHILD: FROM 1 YEAR
FREEZE TIME: 8-10 WEEKS

96

QUICK AND EASY PIZZA

This is a quick, non-yeast pizza. Use a combination of your favourite toppings.

Serves 4-6

225 G/8 OZ SELF-RAISING 85% WHOLEWHEAT FLOUR OR HALF WHOLEMEAL, HALF WHITE FLOUR

1/2 TEASPOON DRY MUSTARD

PINCH OF TEASPOON SALT

2 TEASPOONS BAKING POWDER

4 TABLESPOONS OLIVE OIL

40 G/1 1/2 OZ GRATED CHEESE

150 ML/5 FL OZ MILK OR SOYA MILK AND WATER

For the topping

2 ONIONS, PEELED AND CHOPPED

2 TABLESPOONS OIL

2 TABLESPOONS TOMATO PURÉE

SALT AND FRESHLY GROUND BLACK PEPPER

50 G/2 OZ BUTTON MUSHROOMS OR SLICED TOMATOES

50 G/2 OZ GRATED CHEESE

2 TEASPOONS OREGANO

Set the oven to 220°C/425°F/Gas Mark 7.

Put the flour into a bowl with the mustard powder, salt, baking powder and grated cheese into a bowl, then stir in the oil and milk or water to make soft dough.

Turn the dough on to a floured surface and knead lightly, then roll dough out to fit a large baking sheet or round pizza dish.

Prick the pizza all over, then put it into the oven for 10 minutes while you prepare the topping.

Fry the onions in the oil for 10 minutes, then add the tomato purée and season.

Spread the onion mixture over the pizza base, then put the sliced mushrooms or tomatoes on top. Sprinkle with the grated cheese and oregano.

Put the pizza back into the oven and bake for 20-25 minutes, until puffed up and golden brown on top, then serve.

You can make a very good vegan version as described by using soya milk and vegan cheese.

PREP TIME: 30 MINS
COOKING TIME: 25 MINS
RECOMMENDED AGE OF CHILD: FROM 1 YEAR
FREEZE TIME: 8-10 WEEKS

PANCAKES

These are so quick and easy to make, nutritious and popular with all the children I've known. The pancakes can be sweet or savoury, depending on the filling. Grated or cream cheese (dairy or vegan, in both cases) make quick and popular savoury fillings, as does a thick tomato sauce; maple syrup, honey or one of the healthier sugars such as rapadura make popular sweet choices. They freeze well and if you 'openfreeze' them, spread them out in a single layer until frozen then store in a large container you can take them out one at a time. They take no time at all to thaw.

Makes about 10, depending on thickness.

125G/4 OZ PLAIN FLOUR, PREFERABLY FINE WHOLEMEAL

PINCH OF SALT

2 EGGS

1 TABLESPOON OLIVE OIL OR MELTED BUTTER

300 ML/10 FL OZ MILK OR SOYA MILK AND WATER MIXED

Either put all the ingredients into a blender or food processor and whiz until smooth; or put the flour into a bowl with the salt, make a well in the centre and add the egg, oil and a little of the milk. Beat until smooth, then gradually add the rest of the milk.

Brush a small frying pan with oil. When it's hot enough to sizzle when a drop of water is flicked in, pour in some batter - 2 tablespoons for thin pancakes, more for thick ones, the choice is yours.

Tip the pan so that the batter spreads, then start to lift the edges to see if it's beginning to brown underneath. When it is, and the top is set - just a minute or two - lift it and flip it over with your fingers and a palette knife, and cook the other side, then slide it out onto a plate.

Repeat until you've used all the mixture, piling them up on a plate or serving them to the hungry hordes straight away, with the chosen fillings/toppings.

PREP TIME: 10 MINS

COOKING TIME: 15 MINS

RECOMMENDED AGE OF CHILD: FROM 10 MONTHS

FREEZE TIME: 8-10 WEEKS

Quick ideas:

GLAMORGAN SAUSAGES

Quick to make, crisp little sausages, good with tomato ketchup, a cooked vegetable or a salad. Put 225g/8 oz soft wholemeal breadcrumbs, 175g/6oz grated mild cheese, a small grated onion, a teaspoonful of dried mixed herbs, a tablespoonful of chopped fresh parsley and a teaspoon of Dijon mustard into a bowl and mix. Stir in 1 beaten egg to make a fairly firm consistency. Season with salt and pepper. Form the mixture into about 32 small sausages. Dip the sausages into another beaten egg, then into dried crumbs. Fry the sausages in a little oil, turning them several times, so that they are crisp and golden brown all over and the egg thoroughly cooked. Drain on kitchen paper and serve at once. For a vegan version use grated vegan cheese and egg-replacer, from health shops, instead of the eggs.

SCRAMBLED EGGS

Serves 2-4 people. Beat 4 eggs and season with salt and pepper. Melt a knob of butter in a saucepan and when it sizzles, add the eggs. Cook over a low heat, stirring. For creamy scrambled eggs, remove from the heat just before the eggs set. They will cook a little more in the heat of the pan. If you want firmer scrambled eggs, cook for a moment or two longer, until no longer runny - for children, this is best, to be on the safe side. Serve at once, on to warmed plates and maybe onto hot buttered toast.

SPANISH OMELETTE

This is a quick and easy dish that's popular with all age groups. It's great served hot but if there's any over, it's surprisingly good cold, too. Peel 450g/1 lb potatoes, cut them into 1cm/1/2in chunks and boil in water to cover for 10-15 minutes, or until they feel just tender when tested with the point of a knife. Drain. Heat 2 tablespoons of oil in a large frying pan and fry a chopped onion, uncovered, for 10 minutes, until tender. Heat the grill. Add a crushed garlic clove, the potatoes, 2 tablespoons chopped parsley and eggs to the frying pan and season with salt and pepper. Cook for a few minutes, until set underneath. Then put the pan under the grill for a few minutes to set the top. Cut into sections and serve.

EGGY BREAD

Very useful and nutritious. Whisk an egg and put into a shallow dish. Dip slices of wholemeal bread (preferably with crusts removed) into the egg, letting it soak in a bit, then fry the pieces in a couple of tablespoons of hot olive oil in a frying pan. When lightly browned on one side, flip them over and do the other side. Serve as they are or with fried or grilled tomatoes and mushrooms - or with a little runny honey or maple syrup for a teatime treat.

98

VEGETABLES

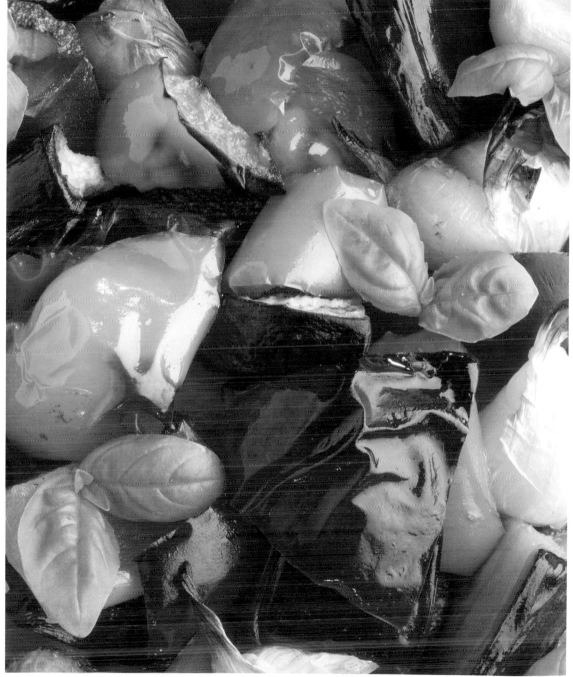

ROASTED ROOT VEGETABLES

These are good served with dal sauce and some cooked millet, rice or quinoa. Also good with hot cooked pasta, and with some green salad and hummus.

Serves 4

350G/12OZ CELERIAC

350G/12OZ PARSNIPS

350G/12OZ YELLOW-FLESHED SWEET POTATOES

350G/12OZ POTATOES

350G/12OZ RED ONIONS

3 TABLESPOONS OLIVE OIL

1 BULB OF GARLIC

Set the oven to 200°C/400°F/Gas Mark 6. Put the olive oil into a roasting tin and put it in the oven to heat up.

Peel the celeriac and parsnips, then cut them into chunks. Scrub the potatoes and sweet potatoes and cut into chunky pieces (no need to peel); peel the onions and cut them into quarters or eighths.

Put the vegetables into the roasting tin, turning them so that they all get coated with oil.

Meanwhile, break the garlic into cloves but don't peel them. Add the garlic to the vegetables after they have been roasting for about 30 minutes, then roast them for a further 25-30 minutes, or until they are golden brown.

PREP TIME: 15 MINS

COOKING TIME: 1 HOUR

RECOMMENDED AGE OF CHILD: FROM 8 MONTHS

FREEZE TIME: UNSUITABLE FOR FREEZING

ROASTED MEDITERRANEAN VEGETABLES

Serve these with some fluffy cooked quinoa and some hummus, with a green salad on the side if you like. Also good with hot cooked pasta.

Serves 2-3

2 LARGE RED PEPPERS

2 LARGE YELLOW PEPPERS

1 AUBERGINE

2 MEDIUM COURGETTES

4 TABLESPOONS OLIVE OIL

4 GARLIC CLOVES, UNPEELED

SALT AND FRESHLY GROUND BLACK PEPPER

Preheat the oven to 230°C/450°F/Gas Mark 8.

Halve, de-seed and slice the peppers; cut the aubergine and courgettes into 1-cm/^{1}/$_2$in chunks.

Put the peppers, aubergine and courgette into a roasting tin with the oil and turn the vegetables with your hands so that they get coated all over with oil.

Bake for 20 minutes, then add the garlic cloves, reduce the setting to 180°C/350°F/Gas Mark 4 and bake for a further 20-30 minutes, until all the vegetables are tender.

Season and serve. You could throw in a few black olives or fresh basil; sometimes I also like to add some drained canned artichoke hearts along with the garlic.

PREP TIME: 15 MINS

COOKING TIME: 1 HOUR

RECOMMENDED AGE OF CHILD: FROM 8 MONTHS

FREEZE TIME: UNSUITABLE FOR FREEZING

TOFU POTATO CAKES

Young children love potato cakes and by mixing the potato with some tofu you can make them into a really nutritious meal. These are best made fresh since tofu doesn't freeze well.

Serves 4

2250G/9OZ POTATOES, PEELED AND CUT INTO EVEN-SIZED CHUNKS

15G /¹/₂OZ BUTTER OR PURE VEGETABLE MARGARINE

A LITTLE MILK OR SOYA MILK

100G/4OZ FIRM TOFU

1-2 TABLESPOONS CHOPPED PARSLEY

SALT AND FRESHLY GROUND BLACK PEPPER

FLOUR

RAPESEED OIL

Boil the potatoes until tender, then drain and mash with the butter or margarine and a little milk or soya milk if necessary.

Mash the tofu, and then add to the potato, along with the parsley and salt and pepper to taste.

Form the mixture into four flat cakes, coat with flour, then either brush with oil and grill on both sides or shallow-fry. Drain on kitchen paper.

PREP TIME: 30 MINS
COOKING TIME: 10 MINS
RCOMMENDED AGE OF CHILD: FROM 1 YEAR
FREEZE TIME: 8-10 WEEKS

QUICK AND EASY POTATO AND CHEESE LAYER

This is very quick and easy to prepare, and popular with children, you just need to allow time for it to cook slowly in the oven. It's nice with a plainly cooked green vegetable or some watercress.

Serves 2-4 as a main course

2 TABLESPOONS OLIVE OIL

2 LARGE POTATOES, PEELED AND THINLY SLICED

2 MEDIUM-SIZED ONIONS, PEELED AND THINLY SLICED

125 G/4 OZ GRATED CHEESE, DAIRY OR VEGAN

4 TABLESPOONS MILK OR SOYA MILK

SALT AND FRESHLY GROUND BLACK PEPPER

Set the oven to 200°C/400°F/Gas Mark 6. Brush a shallow casserole dish with some of the olive oil.

Put a layer of potatoes in the bottom of the dish, then a thin layer of onion slices, a little grated cheese, salt and pepper.

Continue in layers like this until all the ingredients are used, ending with potato.

Pour the milk and remaining olive oil over the top.

Bake for about 1 hour, until crisp and golden on top and the potato feels tender when you insert a sharp knife into the casserole.

PREP TIME: 20 MINS
COOKING TIME: 1-1¹/₄HOURS
RECOMMENDED AGE OF CHILD: FROM 10 MONTHS
FREEZE TIME: NOT APPLICABLE

BIRCHER POTATOES

Quick and delicious, these are like a cross between a baked and a roast potato, easy to do, healthy and loved by everyone. To make enough for 4 people, first set the oven to 200°C/400°F/Gas Mark 6. Scrub 6-8 medium potatoes, organic if possible, and cut in half lengthwise. Brush a baking sheet or roasting tin with oil – I use olive oil, rapeseed or soya oil. Place the potatoes, cut-side down, on the oiled tin and sprinkle with a little sea salt if you like. Bake for about 45 minutes, until the tops feel soft when you press them, and the underneath part is crisp and golden. Serve immediately. My children always liked these with some mint sauce – bought, or home-made from freshly chopped mint mixed with cider vinegar and a dash of clear honey.

102

QUICK AND HEALTHY OVENCHIPS

Every child I know loves chips and frozen oven chips are an easy way to provide them. If, like me, you're not happy about children having that amount of fat on a regular basis, try these. They're really quick to prepare, are made with good quality cooking oil (and not much of it) and don't take long to make. Preheat the oven to 230°C/450°F/Gas Mark 8 and put a baking sheet in the oven to heat up. Peel 350g/12oz potatoes and cut into thickish chips. Sprinkle a tablespoonful of rapeseed or soya oil over them and turn the chips with your hands so that they are all coated with the oil. Then put them on the hot baking sheet in a single layer. Bake for 20 minutes, then turn the chips, and cook for a further 20-30 minutes, turning them again if possible, until they are golden brown and crisp all over. Serve immediately.

This quantity makes enough for 1 adult: the number of children it will serve depends on the age of the child but most children seem to have a huge capacity when it comes to eating chips and this quantity can be multiplied up as necessary. Make sure all the chips are spread out in a single layer though. If they'll eat the chips with a protein-rich dip like hummus, cheese dip, tofu dip, a little pot of lentil soup served as dal, or even some crackers and cheese, or yoghurt for dessert, and maybe a little salad or fruit alongside (or am I pushing my luck here?) this becomes a really healthy meal.

TOFU FLAN

This flan is lovely with cooked green beans, a tomato salad or a green salad.

Serves 4

200G/7OZ PLAIN WHOLEMEAL FLOUR
100G/3¹/₂OZ BUTTER OR VEGAN MARGARINE
3 LARGE ONIONS, PEELED AND SLICED
2 TABLESPOONS OLIVE OIL
250G/9OZ TOFU
4 TABLESPOONS SOYA MILK
2 TEASPOONS DIJON MUSTARD
SALT, PEPPER AND GRATED NUTMEG
6 TEASPOONS OF COLD WATER

Preheat the oven to 200°C/400°F/Gas Mark 6.

Sift the flour and baking powder into a bowl or food processor; add the butter or margarine and whiz, if you're using a food processor, or mix in with a fork or with your fingers until the mixture looks like coarse breadcrumbs. Add 6 teaspoons of cold water and whiz again briefly or press with your fingers to make a ball of dough.

Put the dough on a lightly floured board and pat into a rough circle, then roll it out to fit a

23cm/9in flan dish or tin. Don't worry if it breaks a bit, just patch it up then trim the edges and prick the base.

Bake the flan for 20 minutes until the base is crisp and 'set'.

Meanwhile fry the onions in the olive oil for 10 minutes until really tender; turn up the heat towards the end to let them turn golden.

Put the tofu into a food processor with the soya milk, a heaped tablespoonful of the cooked onion, the mustard and salt, pepper and nutmeg to taste and whiz to a cream.

Spoon the rest of the onions into the flan and spoon the tofu mixture on top. Put the flan back into the oven, turn the heat down to 180°C/350°F/Gas Mark 4 and bake for 25-30 minutes, until the topping if slightly puffed-up and golden brown.

PREP TIME: 45 MINS
COOKING TIME: 45-50 MINS
RECOMMENDED AGE OF CHILD: FROM 1 YEAR
FREEZE TIME: 8-10 WEEKS

QUICK MUSHROOM AND ALMOND NUTMEAT

This recipe, from the first edition of the Baby book, has a somewhat old-fashioned sound to it, but I decided to include it because so many people have asked for it. It's a good source of iron and children and adults like it. I like it with new potatoes and a cooked green vegetable or salad.

Serves 4

150ML/5FL OZ BOILING WATER

1 TEASPOON YEAST EXTRACT

4 SLICES OF WHOLEMEAL BREAD, CRUSTS REMOVED

1 ONION, PEELED AND FINELY CHOPPED

2 TABLESPOONS OIL

125G/4OZ BUTTON MUSHROOMS, WASHED AND SLICED

125G/4OZ ALMONDS, FINELY GRATED IN A COFFEE MILL – OR USE GROUND ALMONDS

1 TABLESPOON SOY SAUCE

1 TABLESPOON LEMON JUICE

SALT AND PEPPER

CHOPPED PARSLEY AND LEMON WEDGES, TO SERVE

Put the boiling water, yeast extract and bread into a bowl. Leave on one side.

Fry the onion in the oil for 7 minutes, browning lightly, then add the mushrooms and fry for 3 minutes more.

Stir in the bread and water mixture, the almonds, soy sauce, lemon juice and seasoning. Mix gently, cook for a few minutes longer to heat everything through, then serve, sprinkled with chopped parsley and garnished with lemon wedges. Some fingers of hot wholewheat toast are pleasant with this if you want a crisp texture to contrast.

PREP TIME: 20 MINS
COOKING TIME: 15 MINS
RECOMMENDED AGE OF CHILD: FROM 1 YEAR
FREEZE TIME: 8-10 WEEKS

EASIEST EVER AUBERGINE, TOMATO AND MOZZARELLA BAKE

This is very quick and easy, and surprisingly popular with children. If there's any left over, it's even better the next day because it seems to thicken up overnight. Green salad or a cooked green vegetable such as broccoli goes well with it – and mashed or jacket potatoes if you want something more substantial.

Serves 4

2 LARGE AUBERGINES, SLICED

OLIVE OIL

690G JAR PASSATA (SIEVE TOMATOES)

2 GARLIC CLOVES, CRUSHED

1/2 TEASPOON DRIED OREGANO

1/2 TEASPOON DRIED THYME

SALT AND FRESHLY GROUND BLACK PEPPER

400G/14OZ MOZZARELLA CHEESE, THINLY SLICED

Heat the grill and set the oven to 200°C/400°F/Gas Mark 6.

Cut the aubergines into 6mm/1/4inch circles and put them on an oiled grill pan. (No need to oil the aubergines for this recipe.) Grill until tender and lightly browned on both sides, turning them half way through.

Stack them up in a pile one on top of the other so that they continue to cook in their own steam for a few minutes while you prepare the sauce.

To do this, simply stir the garlic, oregano and thyme into the tomato passata and season with salt and pepper.

Put a little passata into a shallow gratin dish followed by a layer of aubergine, more passata then a layer of half the mozzarella. Continue with more passata, aubergine and a final layer of mozzarella.

Bake, uncovered, for about 50 minutes until the aubergine feels very tender when you insert a knife, and the top is very well browned.

PREP TIME: 30 MINS

COOKING TIME: 50 MINS

RECOMMENDED AGE OF CHILD: FROM 10 MONTHS

FREEZE TIME: 8-10 WEEKS

QUICK VEGETABLE DISHES

CABBAGE WITH COCONUT

Wash and shred 1 small green cabbage or half a large one. Cook the cabbage in 1cm/1/2in of boiling water in a covered saucepan for about 4 minutes, or until tender. Drain. In another saucepan heat a tablespoonful of oil and fry a chopped onion and a small sliced green chilli until tender: about 10 minutes. Stir in the cabbage along with 1-2 tablespoons unsweetened desiccated coconut. Season and serve.

CREAMY KALE

Kale has a strong flavour which children can find difficult. Try it this German way. Cook 500g/1lb kale in 1cm/1/2in of boiling water for about 7 minutes, or until tender, then drain. Blend 2 teaspoons of wholemeal flour with 150ml/1/4 pint of soya milk and pour into the hot kale. Stir over the heat until the soya mixture has thickened and made a creamy sauce. Season with salt and pepper as required.

104

STUFFED BAKED POTATOES

Allow 1 medium-sized potato per person and 1 or 2 extra. Scrub and prick the potatoes. Put them into a dry baking tin and bake in a hot oven - 230°C/450°F/Gas Mark 8 - for about an hour, until they feel soft when pressed. Holding them with oven gloves or a tea towel, cut each in half and scoop the potato out into a bowl, leaving the skins intact. Then mash the potato with a knob of butter or margarine, some grated cheese and a little milk or soya milk to make a thick, creamy consistency. Season as desired with salt and pepper. Pile the mixture back into the skins, heaping it up - you won't fill all the skins, which was the reason for putting in some extra potatoes. Put the potatoes back into the oven and bake for a further 20-30 minutes, until brown and crisp.

EASY CAULIFLOWER CHEESE

Cut a cauliflower into florets and cook in 1cm/1/2in boiling water for about 5 minutes, or until the cauliflower is tender. Heat the grill. Drain the cauliflower. Put a cupful of cauliflower florets into a food processor with a small carton of smooth white cheese or a little cream and whiz to a creamy purée. Mix this with the rest of the cauliflower and stir in 175g/6oz grated cheese. Season and spoon the mixture into a shallow casserole dish. Sprinkle the top with a little more cheese then pop under the grill until golden brown. Serve with a salad.

PASTA

CONCHIGLIE WITH BROCCOLI CREAM SAUCE

Something soothing and a bit indulgent to sit down to after a tiring evening with the baby... Try it also using asparagus in the summer.

Serves 2-3

25G/1OZ BUTTER OR PURE VEGETABLE MARGARINE

1 ONION, PEELED AND FINELY CHOPPED

1 GARLIC CLOVE, PEELED AND CRUSHED

300ML/10 FL OZ SINGLE CREAM OR SOYA CREAM

250G/9OZ CONCHIGLIE, OR OTHER PASTA SHAPES

350G/12OZ BROCCOLI, WASHED AND CUT INTO FAIRLY SMALL PIECES

1 TEASPOON CORNFLOUR

1-2 TABLESPOONS LEMON JUICE

SALT AND FRESHLY GROUND BLACK PEPPER

GRATED NUTMEG

Put a large pan of water on the stove to heat for the pasta.

Melt the butter or margarine in a small saucepan, and add the onion and garlic; cover and cook gently until the onion is tender but not brown, 5-10 minutes.

Pour in most of the cream, keeping enough back to make a paste with the cornflour. Leave the mixture to simmer gently for about 5 minutes, until the cream has thickened a bit.

Blend the cornflour with the remaining cream and add. Stir until the sauce has thickened even more, cook for 1 minute, and then remove from the heat.

Cook the pasta in the boiling water according to packet instructions, or for about 8 minutes, until it's al dente, then drain it and return to the pan. Stir in the remaining tablespoon of oil and salt and pepper to taste.

Meanwhile cook the broccoli in a little boiling water until just tender – check after 3-4 minutes. Drain and add to the sauce, with lemon juice (especially if you're using soya cream, which is slightly sweet), salt, pepper and nutmeg to taste.

Either mix the sauce in with the spaghetti and serve, or serve the spaghetti out onto plates and spoon the sauce over. Either way, top with grated cheese and /or torn basil.

PREP AND COOKING TIME: 30 MINS

RECOMMENDED AGE OF CHILD: FROM 10 MONTHS

FREEZE TIME: As a dish I do not recommend freezing this, however, separately the sauce does freeze well

PENNE WITH MEDITERRANEAN SAUCE

Serves 2

2 TABLESPOONS OLIVE OIL

1 ONION, PEELED AND CHOPPED

1 GARLIC CLOVE, PEELED AND CRUSHED

1 RED PEPPER, DE-SEEDED AND CHOPPED

1 AUBERGINE, CUT INTO 5MM/¼INCH DICE

400G /14 OZ CAN CHOPPED TOMATOES IN JUICE

SALT AND FRESHLY GROUND BLACK PEPPER

GRATED FRESH PARMESAN-STYLE CHEESE OR VEGAN PARMESAN TO SERVE

Put a large pan of water on the stove to heat for the pasta.

Heat the oil in a fairly large pan, and put in the onion, garlic, red pepper and aubergine. Stir, cover and leave to cook gently for 10 minutes.

Add the tomatoes, bring to the boil, and simmer gently, uncovered, until all the liquid has disappeared: 15-20 minutes. Season with salt and pepper.

Meanwhile cook the pasta in the boiling water according to packet instructions, or for about 8 minutes, until it's al dente, then drain it and return to the pan. Stir in the remaining tablespoon of oil and salt and pepper to taste.

Either mix the sauce in with the pasta and serve, or serve the pasta out onto plates and spoon the sauce over. Serve with Parmesan-style cheese.

PREP AND COOKING TIME: 30 MINS

RECOMMENDED AGE OF CHILD: FROM 10 MONTHS

FREEZE TIME: As a dish I do not recommend freezing this but separately the sauce does freeze well. Cool the sauce, then pour into a suitable container and freeze. To use, thaw, then reheat gently

WHOLEMEAL SPAGHETTI WITH QUICK TOMATO SAUCE AND GRATED CHEESE

A perennial favourite which children love. You may need to purée the sauce if your kids don't like 'bits'. I think it's lovely made with wholemeal pasta, but do feel free to disagree and use your favourite type.

Serves 2

2 TABLESPOONS OLIVE OIL

1 ONION, CHOPPED

1-2 GARLIC CLOVES, CHOPPED

400G/14OZ CAN TOMATOES

1 TABLESPOON TOMATO PURÉE OR SUNDRIED TOMATO PURÉE

250G/9OZ SPAGHETTI

SALT AND FRESHLY GROUND BLACK PEPPER

TO SERVE: FRESHLY GRATED PARMESAN-STYLE CHEESE AND/OR TORN BASIL LEAVES

Put a large pan of water on the stove to heat up for the spaghetti. Heat 1 tablespoon of the oil in a pan, add the onion, then cover and cook gently for 10 minutes. Add the garlic and stir for a moment, then add the tomatoes, chopping them up with a spoon. Leave it to simmer, uncovered for 10-15 minutes, until the liquid has reduced a little.

Cook the spaghetti in the boiling water according to packet instructions, or for about 8 minutes, until it's al dente, then drain it and return to the pan. Stir in the remaining tablespoon of oil and salt and pepper to taste.

Either mix the sauce in with the spaghetti and serve, or serve the spaghetti out onto plates and spoon the sauce over. Either way, top with grated cheese and /or torn basil.

PREP AND COOKING TIME: 30 MINS

RECOMMENDED AGE OF CHILD: FROM 10 MONTHS

FREEZE TIME: This sauce freezes well: pour into a suitable lidded container, allowing room for the sauce to expand as it freezes. It can be stored for 8-10 weeks

SPAGHETTI WITH LENTIL SAUCE

Serves 2

2 TABLESPOONS OLIVE OIL

1 ONION, CHOPPED

1-2 GARLIC CLOVES, CHOPPED

250G/8OZ CAN TOMATOES

1 TABLESPOON TOMATO PURÉE OR SUNDRIED TOMATO PURÉE

425G/14OZ CAN GREEN LENTILS, DRAINED AND RINSED

250G/9OZ SPAGHETTI

SALT AND FRESHLY GROUND BLACK PEPPER

TO SERVE: FRESHLY GRATED PARMESAN-STYLE CHEESE AND/OR TORN BASIL LEAVES

Put a large pan of water on the stove to heat up for the spaghetti.

Heat 1 tablespoon of the oil in a pan, add the onion, then cover and cook gently for 10 minutes. Add the garlic and stir for a moment, then add the tomatoes, chopping them up with a spoon. Stir in the lentils and tomato purée, then simmer, uncovered for 10-15 minutes, until the liquid has reduced a little.

Cook the spaghetti in the boiling water according to packet instructions, or for about 8 minutes, until it's al dente, then drain it and return to the pan. Stir in the remaining tablespoon of oil and salt and pepper to taste.

Either mix the sauce in with the spaghetti and serve, or serve the spaghetti out onto plates and spoon the sauce over. Either way, top with grated cheese and /or torn basil.

PREP AND COOKING TIME: 45 MINS
RECOMMENDED AGE OF CHILD: FROM 10 MONTHS
FREEZE TIME: The sauce can be frozen separately for 8-10 weeks

PENNE WITH SPINACH AND RICOTTA

Serves 2

250G/9OZ PENNE

225G/8OZ BABY SPINACH LEAVES

1-2 TABLESPOONS OLIVE OIL

125G/4OZ RICOTTA, OR CREAMY SOFT WHITE DAIRY OR VEGAN CHEESE

SALT, PEPPER AND GRATED NUTMEG

Put a large pan of water on the stove to heat for the pasta.

Cook the pasta in the boiling water according to packet instructions, or for about 8 minutes, until it's al dente. Just before it's ready, add the spinach leaves to the pan and cook them for about 1 minute, until wilted. Drain the pasta and spinach together into a colander.

Put the pasta and spinach back into the saucepan along with the oil. Crumble in the ricotta and add salt, pepper and nutmeg. Stir over the heat for a minute or two to warm and slightly melt the cheese, then check the seasoning and serve.

PREP AND COOKING TIME: 30 MINS
RECOMMENDED AGE OF CHILD: FROM 10 MONTHS
FREEZE TIME: FREEZING NOT RECOMMENDED

109

QUICK MACARONI CHEESE

Macaroni cheese is always popular with children but many recipes, I find, are too stodgy. This is a nice light one.

Serves 4

125G/4OZ MACARONI, PREFERABLY WHOLEMEAL

50G/2OZ BUTTER OR MARGARINE

40G/1½OZ WHOLEMEAL FLOUR

600ML/1PINT DAIRY OR SOYA MILK

175G/6OZ CHEDDAR CHEESE, GRATED

½TEASPOON MUSTARD POWDER - OMIT IF MAKING THIS FOR CHILDREN UNDER ONE

SALT AND PEPPER

50G/2OZ SOFT WHOLEMEAL BREADCRUMBS

Preheat the oven to 200°C/400°F/Gas Mark 6.

Cook the macaroni in plenty of boiling water until just tender; drain.

Meanwhile make a sauce. Put the butter or margarine, flour and milk into a saucepan and whisk over the heat for about 5 minutes, until smooth and creamy.

Remove from the heat and stir in the drained pasta, most of the cheese, mustard and salt and pepper to taste. Pour into a shallow casserole, top with the crumbs and the rest of the cheese and bake for 30-40 minutes, until golden brown.

PREP TIME: 40 MINS

COOKING TIME: 30-40 MINS

RECOMMENDED AGE OF CHILD: FROM 8 MONTHS

FREEZE TIME: 8-10 WEEKS

SPINACH LASAGNE

This is a brilliant way of getting children to 'eat their greens'. It's not instant to make, though not at all difficult; but it is worth making double, and freezing one. You don't have to cook the lasagne before using it, but it's not a lot of trouble to do so and it does give a lighter result.

Serves 4

225G/8OZ LASAGNE SHEETS

500G/1LB SPINACH LEAVES

15G/¹/₂OZ BUTTER OR MARGARINE

225G/8OZ RICOTTA OR SOFT WHITE VEGAN CHEESE

50G/2OZ FRESH PARMESAN-STYLE CHEESE, GRATED, OR VEGAN PARMESAN

1 QUANTITY OF TOMATO SAUCE, P.72

125G/4OZ MOZZARELLA CHEESE, GRATED

Preheat the oven to 190°C/375°F/Gas Mark 5.

Cook the pasta in the boiling water according to packet instructions, until it's al dente, then drain, rinse under cold water and drape the pieces over the rim of a colander or saucepan to prevent them sticking together.

Rinse the spinach then put it into a saucepan with just the water clinging to it and cook for about 5 minutes, or until tender. Drain into a colander, then put it back into the pan with the butter, ricotta, most of the Parmesan-style cheese and some salt and pepper to taste. Mix well.

Put a little of the tomato sauce in the base of a shallow casserole dish then cover with sheets of lasagne. Cover with half of the spinach mixture, a third of the Mozzarella and a quarter of the tomato sauce. Cover with more lasagne then repeat the layers - tomato sauce, spinach, Mozzarella. Put more lasagne on top, spread over the rest of the tomato sauce, and then sprinkle with Mozzarella and the remaining Parmesan-style cheese.

PREP TIME: 40 MINS

COOKING TIME: Bake for about 30-35 minutes, until golden brown and crisp on top

RECOMMENDED AGE OF CHILD: FROM 8 MONTHS

FREEZE TIME: 8-10 WEEKS

PUDDINGS, CAKES AND SWEETS THINGS

MOLASSES FLAPJACKS

A healthy version of an old favourite.

Makes 16

50G/2OZ BLACK TREACLE OR MOLASSES

50G/2OZ BARBADOS OR MUSCOVADO SUGAR

8 TABLESPOONS RAPESEED OIL

250G/9OZ ROLLED OATS

50G/2OZ SUNFLOWER SEEDS

Set the oven to 180°C/350°F/Gas Mark 4.

Put the treacle or molasses, the sugar and oil into a medium saucepan and heat gently.

When the sugar has dissolved, remove from the heat and stir in the oats and sunflower seeds.

Pour the mixture into a greased shallow tin, 18 x 28 cm/7 x 11 inches, press down and bake towards the top of the oven for 20-25 minutes, or until it's set, crisp round the edges and the visible oats are golden brown.

Cool slightly, then mark into sections with a knife and leave in the tin to cool completely.

PREP TIME: 15 MINS

COOKING TIME: 20-25 MINS

RECOMMENDED AGE OF CHILD: FROM 1 YEAR

FREEZE TIME: Can be frozen but equally keeps well in a tin for at least a week

GINGERBREAD MEN

Another one for when you feel like having a weighing, mixing, rolling and cutting session in the kitchen.... This is a splendid plain ginger biscuit mixture that stands up to a lot of rolling and re-rolling and tastes good too, though in my experience it's the making that's the most fun...You can make these vegan by using egg substitute powder (from health shops) to the equivalent 1 egg. You can also get agave syrup at good heath shops - it's a healthier sweetener than golden syrup and tastes gorgeous.

50G/2OZ GOLDEN SYRUP OR AGAVE SYRUP

300G/10OZ PLAIN FLOUR - WHITE, FINE WHOLEMEAL OR A MIXTURE

1 TEASPOON BAKING POWDER

1 TEASPOONS GROUND GINGER

125G/4OZ SOFT BUTTER OR MARGARINE

125G/4OZ RAPADURA OR OTHER SOFT BROWN SUGAR

1 EGG, BEATEN

1-2 TABLESPOONS MILK OR WATER, OPTIONAL

Preheat the oven to 160°C/325°F/Gas Mark 3. Put the syrup into a small saucepan and warm over the heat to make it more liquid. Set aside.

Sift the flour, baking powder and ginger into a bowl. Add the butter or margarine and rub in with your fingers until you can't see any pieces any more. Stir in the sugar, then the egg or egg replacement, and the melted syrup.

Mix to a fairly sticky dough, adding a little milk or water if necessary. It needs to be firm enough to roll out but also soft enough so that you can use plenty of flour to roll it out, and to allow for re-rolling the scraps.

Roll the mixture about 6mm/^{1}/4in thick and cut into gingerbread men or whatever shapes you wish - children's pastry sets often contain cutters for animals, and these are fun.

Put the biscuits onto a lightly greased baking tray and bake for about 15 minutes. Check them just before to see how they're doing. They need to feel 'set' but not hard, as they'll harden up as they

112

cool. Don't overcook them – they won't hurt if they're very slightly underdone.

Cool on a wire rack.

PREP TIME: 20 MINS

COOKING TIME: 15 MINS

RECOMMENDED AGE OF CHILD: FROM 1 YEAR TO EAT; FROM ABOUT 3 TO MAKE, WITH LOTS OF HELP

FREEZE TIME: 8-10 WEEKS

EASY FRUIT CAKE

So easy to make: just a bit of measuring and mixing. The result is a wonderful, moist, old-fashioned fruitcake, packed with nutritious goodies. It keeps well in a tin.

Makes a 20cm/8in cake

350G/12OZ PLAIN WHOLEMEAL FLOUR

1 TEASPOON GROUND MIXED SPICE

150 ML /5 FL OZ GROUNDNUT OIL

175G/6OZ MOLASSES SUGAR

225G/8OZ MIXED DRIED FRUIT

100 G/4OZ GLACÉ CHERRIES, RINSED AND HALVED

GRATED RIND OF 1 ORGANIC ORANGE

25G/1OZ GROUND ALMONDS

125ML/4FL OZ MILK OR SOYA MILK

2 TABLESPOONS VINEGAR

3/4 TEASPOON BICARBONATE OF SODA

25G/1OZ FLAKED ALMONDS, OPTIONAL

Set the oven to 150°C/300°F/Gas Mark 2. Grease a 20cm/8 inch cake tin and line with a double layer of greaseproof or non-stick paper.

Sift the flour and spice into a bowl, adding the bran from the sieve too. Stir in the oil, sugar, dried

fruit, cherries, orange rind, and ground almonds and mix until combined.

Warm half the milk in a small saucepan and add the vinegar. Dissolve the bicarbonate of soda in the rest of the milk, then add to the milk and vinegar mixture and pour into the flour and fruit, blending well.

Spoon into the prepared cake tin and scatter the almonds on top if you're using them. Bake for 2-2 1/2 hours, until a skewer inserted into the centre of the cake comes out clean.

Leave to cool in the tin, then strip off the paper.

PREP TIME: 20 MINS

COOKING TIME: 2 - 2 1/2 HOURS

RECOMMENDED AGE OF CHILD: FROM 1 YEAR

NOTE: KEEPS WELL IN A TIN FOR AT LEAST 2 WEEKS

QUICK CHOCOLATE CAKE

This is a basic quick cake mixture that children like. They like eating it but most of all they like making it, with lots of bowl licking at the end. You can let them do this with an easy mind because the recipe is eggless, so no worries about salmonella. The texture, however, is light – and a bit crumbly. We all like the chocolate version best, though for a plain cake you can leave the cocoa out and increase the flour by 50g/2oz. You can get rapadura sugar (a lovely healthy brown sugar) from good health shops.

Makes one 18cm/7in cake

175G/6OZ SELF-RAISING FLOUR: WHITE, WHOLEMEAL OR A MIXTURE

50G/2OZ COCOA POWDER

2 TEASPOONS BAKING POWDER

175G/6OZ CASTER OR RAPADURA SUGAR

113

6 TABLESPOONS RAPESEED OR OLIVE OIL, OR MELTED
BUTTER

225ML/8OZ WATER

1 TEASPOON REAL VANILLA EXTRACT (OR VANILLA
ESSENCE)

Preheat the oven to 180°C/350°F/Gas Mark 4.
Grease and base-line two 18cm/7in sandwich
tines.

Sift the flour, cocoa and baking powder into a
bowl. Add the sugar, then stir in the oil or melted
butter, water and vanilla essence.

Mix to a smooth, batter-like consistency; pour
into the tins.

Bake for 25-30 minutes, until the centre springs
back to a light touch. Let them cool in the tins for
a few minutes, then turn out onto a wire rack.
Remove the paper when they're cold and
sandwich and ice with the buttercream.

To make the buttercream just beat together
50g/2oz soft butter or vegetable margarine,
125g/4oz icing sugar or rapadura sugar, a
tablespoonful of cocoa powder, half a teaspoon
of vanilla essence and a few drops of hot water,
as necessary, to make a creamy consistency.

QUICK BUNS

The chocolate cake mixture also makes excellent
buns. To make about 12, halve all the quantities
and make as described. Spoon or pour the
mixture into paper cake cases, then bake for 10-
15 minutes, or until they spring back when
touched.

PREP TIME: 20 MINS

COOKING TIME: 10-30 MINS

RECOMMENDED AGE OF CHILD: FROM 1 YEAR, TO EAT; FROM
ABOUT 3 TO MAKE, WITH LOTS OF HELP

FREEZE TIME: 8-10 WEEKS

NUTTY CAROB BANANAS

These are rather like healthy ice creams. If you
are giving them to young children, either use
very finely chopped nuts or leave the nuts out.
You can also make this recipe with pieces of ripe
peach or pear; cut into suitably sized pieces and
remove skin before dipping in honey. Suitable
for children of 1 year onwards as long as you
powder the nuts finely (or leave them out).

CLEAR HONEY

CAROB POWDER

FINELY CHOPPED MIXED NUTS

1 BANANA PER PERSON, PEELED AND CUT INTO 3
EQUAL PIECES

Put the honey, carob powder and chopped nuts
on three saucers.

Dip each piece of banana first into the honey,
then into the carob powder, and finally into the
nuts, so that it is well coated.

Put the banana pieces onto a flat plate or tray
and freeze until solid - this will take about 2
hours or more.

Eat straight from the freezer. You can insert lolly
sticks into the pieces of banana before freezing if
you like.

PARKIN

A sweet sticky cake that children love. It gets
stickier if you keep it for a few days, wrapped in
foil.

Makes 12-16 pieces

100G/4OZ PLAIN WHOLEMEAL FLOUR

2 TEASPOONS BAKING POWDER

2 TEASPOONS GROUND GINGER

100G/4OZ MEDIUM OATMEAL

100G/4OZ MOLASSES SUGAR

100G/4OZ BLACK MOLASSES

100G/4OZ HONEY OR GOLDEN SYRUP

100G/4OZ BUTTER OR PURE VEGETABLE MARGARINE

175ML/6FL OZ MILK OR SOYA MILK

Set the oven to 180°C/350°F/Gas Mark 4. Line a 20cm/8 inch square tin with greased greaseproof paper.

Sift the flour, baking powder and ginger into a bowl, adding the bran left in the sieve, and also the oatmeal.

Put the sugar, molasses, honey or golden syrup, and butter or margarine into a saucepan and heat gently until melted. Cool until you can comfortably put your hand against the pan, then add the milk or soya milk.

Add the treacle mixture to the dry ingredients, mixing well, and pour into the prepared tin.

Bake for 50-60 minutes, until firm to the touch. Lift the parkin out of the tin and put on a wire tray to cool, then cut into pieces and remove from the paper.

PREP TIME: 20 MINS
COOKING TIME: 30-60 MINS
RECOMMENDED AGE OF CHILD: FROM 1 YEAR
NOTE: KEEPS WELL IN A TIN OR WRAPPED IN FOIL FOR UP TO 2 WEEKS

RHUBARB CRUMBLE

Serves 4-6

900G/2LB RHUBARB CUT INTO 2.5CM / 1 INCH LENGTHS

250G/9OZ SUGAR

250G/9OZ SELF-RAISING BROWN OR WHOLEMEAL FLOUR

175G/6OZ BUTTER OR PURE VEGETABLE MARGARINE

Set the oven to 200°C/400°F/Gas Mark 6.

Put the rhubarb in an even layer in a lightly greased large shallow casserole. Sprinkle 75g/3oz of the sugar on top.

Put the flour into a bowl and rub in the butter with your fingertips until the mixture looks like fine breadcrumbs. Stir in the rest of the sugar.

Spoon the crumble topping on top of the rhubarb.

Bake for about 40 minutes until the crumble is crisp and lightly browned and the fruit feels tender when pierced with a skewer.

PREP TIME: 15 MINS
COOKING TIME: 40 MINS
RECOMMENDED AGE OF CHILD: FROM 1 YEAR
FREEZE TIME: 8-10 WEEKS

MILLET AND RAISIN CREAM

The old-fashioned milk puddings that our grandmothers used to make were nutritionally excellent, as well as economical. This up-to-date version is based on protein and iron-rich flaked millet, with raisins for sweetness.

Serves 3-4

125G/4OZ FLAKED MILLET

600ML/1 PINT MILK OR SOYA MILK

50G/2OZ RAISINS

GRATED LEMON RIND (OPTIONAL)

1-2 TABLESPOONS HONEY (OPTIONAL)

Put all the ingredients into a saucepan and bring

to the boil. Reduce the heat to as low as possible and simmer very gently for 20-30 minutes, or until it has thickened.

Serve hot or pour into individual serving dishes and leave to cool. It's good with some single cream or soya cream on top.

PREP AND COOKING TIME: ABOUT 30 MINS

RECOMMENDED AGE OD CHILD: FROM 8 MONTHS (12 MONTHS IF USING HONEY)

FREEZING NOT RECOMMENDED

HEALTHY ICE CREAM

All children love this. It freezes very hard so it needs to be left at room temperature for 45-60 minutes.

Serves 8

900ML/1¹/2 PINTS MILK OR SOYA MILK

100G/4OZ PLAIN CHOCOLATE, BROKEN INTO PIECES

2 ROUNDED TABLESPOONS CASTER SUGAR

1 TABLESPOON CUSTARD POWDER OR CORNFLOUR

400G/14OZ CAN EVAPORATED MILK OR SOYA CREAM

Put all but 4 tablespoons of the milk into a large saucepan with the chocolate and sugar and bring slowly to the boil.

In a bowl, mix the custard powder or cornflour to a paste with the remaining milk. Add a little of the boiling milk to the custard mixture, stir, then pour the mixture into the hot milk.

Stir over the heat for 2-3 minutes until it has thickened a little, and then remove from the heat. Add the evaporated milk or soya cream and blend until smooth.

Pour into a plastic container, cool completely, and freeze until half set. Beat well, and freeze until firm.

PREP TIME: 15 MINS

FREEZING TIME: 2 HOURS OR MORE

RECOMMENDED AGE OF CHILD: FROM 8 MONTHS

APRICOT FOOL

This is easy to make and rich in both iron and calcium - an excellent pudding for babies if you omit the almonds. Organic apricots may not look as beautiful as those that have been preserved with sulphur dioxide, but they have a wonderful brown-sugar flavour.

Serves 3

225G/8OZ ORGANIC DRIED APRICOTS

250G/9OZ THICK GREEK YOGHURT OR SOYA YOGHURT

CLEAR HONEY OR DEMERARA SUGAR

FLAKED ALMONDS (OPTIONAL)

Cover the apricots with boiling water and soak overnight.

The next day, simmer for 20-30 minutes, or until tender.

Cool, then purée in a food processor. Fold the yoghurt or soya yoghurt into the apricot purée and sweeten with honey or sugar to taste.

Serve in small bowls with some flaked almonds on top if you're using these. If you wish, you can make this creamier by replacing some of the yoghurt with whipped cream.

PREP TIME: 30 MINS PLUS OVERNIGHT SOAKING

RECOMMENDED AGE OF CHILD: FROM 6 MONTHS (12 MONTHS IF USING HONEY)

FREEZE TIME: UNSUITABLE FOR FREEZING

116

VARIATIONS

For Mango Fool, use a very ripe mango. Remove the stone, peel and purée the flesh. Mix with yoghurt, soya yoghurt or yoghurt and cream as above.

For Blackberry Fool, just mash very ripe blackberries and fold into yoghurt or yoghurt and cream as above.

SOME EASY COOKED FRUIT IDEAS

BAKED APPLES WITH RAISINS

Easy, nutritious and delicious served with some chilled plain yoghurt. Remove the core from one baking apple per person and stuff raisins, sultanas, dates or brown sugar into the hole. Score around the centre with a sharp knife, just piercing the skin to prevent bursting. Place on an ovenproof dish in an oven set to 200°C/400°F/Gas Mark 6 and bake for 45 minutes, until soft. Lovely either hot or cold.

RECOMMENDED AGE OF CHILD: FROM 8 MONTHS

BAKED PEACHES

Halve ripe (unpeeled) peaches, one per person, and remove the stones. Put them, cut-side down, in a buttered baking dish and sprinkle with demerara sugar. Bake at 180°C/350°F/Gas Mark 4 for about 25 minutes, until they can be pierced easily with a knife.

RECOMMENDED AGE OF CHILD: FROM 8 MONTHS

BAKED BANANAS

Simply put whole, unpeeled bananas in a baking tray and bake at 180°C/350°F/Gas Mark 4 until you can pierce them easily with a knife – about 25-30 minutes. Serve immediately. Thick yoghurt or vanilla ice cream also goes well with them. For a more luxurious version, remove a section of skin from the top of each banana before baking, make some cuts in the banana and insert some slim squares of chocolate. Bake as before. Again, excellent with vanilla ice cream – or whipped cream.

RECOMMENDED AGE OF CHILD: FROM 8 MONTHS

APPLES WITH RAISINS

Melt 225g/1oz of butter or margarine in a heavy-bottomed saucepan and add 900g/2lb of sweet eating apples, such as Cox's, and 50g/2oz raisins or chopped cooking dates (not sugar-rolled). Stir, cover and cook gently for about 10 minutes, or until the apples are soft. Stir from time to time to prevent it burning.

In this recipe the dried fruit adds extra food value (iron and B vitamins) as well as sweetness, so that little or no extra sweetening is needed. If this is sieved or puréed after cooking, it makes an excellent dessert for babies. To freeze, allow to cool quickly, spoon into a suitable covered container, and place in the freezer. Before use, leave to thaw for several hours at room temperature, then either heat gently or serve cold with some single cream.

RECOMMENDED AGE OF CHILD: FROM 6 MONTHS

117

DRIED FRUIT COMPOTE

Put 100g/4oz each of dried figs, apricots, dates and prunes or dried peaches into a bowl. Cover with boiling water, making sure that the fruit is covered. Leave for at least 12 hours; it will keep for several days, covered, in the fridge. It's nice with some fresh fruit added before serving: segments of orange, with the pith cut away, are good; so are slices of kiwi fruit, apple and banana.

RECOMMENDED AGE OF CHILD: FROM 8 MONTHS

FRESH FRUIT IDEAS

BANANA SMOOTHIE

Not really a pudding, but it fits into this section. Put a peeled and roughly chopped banana into a blender or food processor with some milk or soya milk and a tablespoonful of ground almonds and whiz to a cream. For extra iron and calcium, you could also include a heaped teaspoonful of blackstrap molasses.

RECOMMENDED AGE OF CHILD: FROM 1 YEAR

LYCHEES AND KIWI FRUIT

Remove the shell-like skin from the lychees (or use canned lychees) and mix with slices of skinned kiwi fruit. Slices of orange or satsuma are good, too.

RECOMMENDED AGE OF CHILD. FROM 8 MONTHS

EXOTIC FRUIT

Mix together two or more types, depending on what you like, what is available and what is really ripe: juicy mango, paw paw and persimmon are all good. I prefer canned guavas to fresh - these could be added, too, and some pretty cape gooseberries, with the dried sepals pulled back like petals.

RECOMMENDED AGE OF CHILD: FROM 8 MONTHS

BIG C FRUIT SALAD

This refreshing fruit salad or starter can give you a vitamin C boost of around 300mg. You could increase the vitamin C further by making this as a salad rather than a pudding and add sliced red pepper (just 100g/4oz will give you around another 200mg of vitamin C) and/or chicory which is also an excellent source of this vitamin. To make enough for one person, cut the peel from 1 orange and 1 grapefruit and remove the flesh from the segments, holding the fruit over a bowl to catch all the juice. Thinly peel a kiwi fruit, then slice that into the bowl too. Mix and serve.

RECOMMENDED AGE OF CHILD: FROM 1 YEAR

FIGS WITH YOGHURT AND SESAME SEEDS

This useful pudding or breakfast dish supplies over half the recommended daily calcium allowance during pregnancy. Simply mix 100g/4oz chopped dried figs with 150ml/5 fl oz natural dairy or vitamin-enriched soya yoghurt and sprinkle over 1 rounded tablespoon sesame seeds.

RECOMMENDED AGE OF CHILD: FROM 1 YEAR

118

FRESH FRUIT WITH APRICOT SAUCE

Soak and cook dried apricots as for Apricot Fool (p.116). Purée them, adding enough of their liquid to get a pouring consistency and serve over slices of fresh fruit - apples, pears, oranges, bananas. This sauce is delicious and provides useful iron, vitamin A and calcium.

RECOMMENDED AGE OF CHILD: FROM 1 YEAR

BANANAS WITH GINGER

Peel and slice fresh bananas; top with a little chopped preserved ginger, a spoonful of the ginger syrup and perhaps a few crushed nuts.

RECOMMENDED AGE OF CHILD: FROM 5 YEARS (if they like ginger!)

General Index

Recipe Index

125

Useful Addresses

ASSOCIATION OF BREASTFEEDING MOTHERS (ABM) PO Box 207, Bridgwater, Somerset TA6 7YT Tel: 020 7813 1481 www.abm.me.uk

BREASTFEEDING NETWORK PO Box 11126, Paisley PA2 8YB. Breastfeeding counsellors nationwide. Supporter Line 0870 900 8787 www.breastfeedingnetwork.org.uk

ASSOCIATION FOR IMPROVEMENTS IN THE MATERNITY SERVICES (AIMS) 5 Ann's Court, Grove Road, Surbiton, Surrey KT6 4BE. Helpline 0870 765 1433. Support and information about maternity rights and options. List of home birth support groups and independent midwives and local groups. www.aims.org.uk

SERENE (incorporating Cry-sis) London WC1N 3XX. Helpline 020 7404 5011 (9am-10pm); self-help and support for parents of crying, sleepless or higher-need babies.

LA LECHE LEAGUE (Great Britain) PO Box 29, West Bridgford, Nottingham NG2 7NP. Tel: 020 7242 1278. 24 hours breastfeeding information and support through local groups and telephone counselling. www.laleche.org.uk

MATERNITY ALLIANCE Third Floor West 2-6 Northburgh St, London, EC1V 0AY. Info Line 0207 490 7638. Alliance of maternity groups; information about rights at work, maternity benefit, general health and employment benefit.

MEET-A-MUM ASSOCIATION (MAMA) 26 Avenue Road, South Norwood, London WE25 4DX, (office, 9am-5pm) Helpline: 01761 433598. www.mama.org.uk. Information and groups to support women who are isolated, lonely or suffering from postnatal depression; also families. Puts sufferers in touch with others who have had the same experience.

NATIONAL CHILDBIRTH TRUST (NCT) Alexandra House, Oldham Terrace, London W3 6NH. Enquiry line: 0870 444 8707. www.nctpregnancyandbabycare.com. Antenatal classes, postnatal support, breastfeeding counselling, information, study days, leaflets and merchandise. Branches nationwide.

NEW WAYS TO WORK 1-3 Berry St, London, EC1V 0AA. Tel: 0207 253 5358. Information for individuals and employers about flexible work patterns, including sabbaticals, job sharing, voluntary reduced work time, working from home. Book Balanced Lives: Changing Work Patterns for Men, £9.95.

WORKING FAMILIES (formerly Parents at Work) 1-3 Berry St, London, EC1V 0AA. Tel: 0207 253 7243. Information for working parents, including childcare options. www.parentsatwork.org.uk

NHS DIRECT Tel: 0845 4647 Can put you in touch with your local health information service for information on health matters: help to find or change any professional, make a complaint or contact a selfhelp group; details of Maternity Services Patient's Charter.

VEGAN SOCIETY Donald Watson House, 7 Battle Road, St Leonard's on Sea, East Sussex TN37 7AA Tel: 0142 442 7393 Advice on vegan diet during pregnancy Office hours Mon-Fri. 09.00-17.00. www.vegansociety.com

THE VEGETARIAN SOCIETY Parkdale, Dunham Road, Altrincham, Cheshire WA14 4QG Tel: 0161 925 2000. Information on diet during pregnancy. www.vegsoc.org

VIVA! 8 York Court, Wilder St, Bristol, Avon BS2 8QH. Tel: 0117 944 1000 www.viva.org.uk. Advice on vegetarian diet during pregnancy and lively informative booklets on vegetarian/vegan issues

WELLBEING 27 Sussex Place, Regent's Park, London NW1 4SP Tel: 0207 772 6400 Information on nutrition in pregnancy, prematurity, early miscarriage and early diagnosis of foetal abnormalities. Eating in pregnancy helpline: 0845 130 3646 www.wellbeing.org.uk

SOIL ASSOCIATION Bristol House, 40-56 Victoria St, Bristol. BS1 6BY. Tel: 0117 929 0661. For information about organic product, box schemes etc. www.soilassociation.org

ROSE ELLIOT HOROSCOPES Alongside my cookery writing, I work as an astrologer. Some years ago my husband and I collaborated to produce really good computer horoscopes at a reasonable cost. Our child profiles have proved very popular with parents (and grandparents) who find them helpful in understanding the unique qualities which make their baby special. For details of these, and our other services, please write to: Rose Elliot Horoscopes, PO Box 16, Eastleigh, Hampshire SO50 5YP

Further Reading

PREGNANCY AND BIRTH by Gill Thorn (Hamlyn 2000). Gill was my birth counsellor when I had my daughter Claire so I was lucky enough to experience her excellent advice first hand. She was also the consultant on pregnancy and birth for this book. Highly recommended.

PREGNANCY, CHILDREN AND THE VEGAN DIET by Michael Klaper MD (c/o PO Box 959, Felton, Ca, USA). Useful advice from America's leading expert in vegan nutrition.

NOT TOO LATE: HAVING A BABY OVER 35 by Gill Thorn (Bantam 1998). Provides straightforward information and practial advice about pregnancy, birth and parenthood. Highly recommended.

REDISCOVERING BIRTH by Sheila Kitzinger (Little, Brown, 2000). A beautifully illustrated book that asks some searching questions about birth.

HAVE THE BIRTH YOU WANT by Gill Thorn (Hodder and Stoughton 2002). Written for women who want to stay in control and not get swept along by other people's decisions.

BABY AND CHILD by Penelope Leach (Penguin, 1989). Sensitive, practical and informative. My favourite book on childcare.

BESTFEEDING: GETTING BREASTFEEDING RIGHT FOR YOU by Mary Renfrew, Chloe Fisher and Suzanne Arms (Celestial Arts, 1990). An excellent book on breastfeeding.

WHAT TO EXPECT WHEN YOU'RE BREASTFEEDING....AND WHAT IF YOU CAN'T by Clare Byam-Cook (Vermilion 2001). Sound advice and reassurance.

THE WORKING PARENTS HANDBOOK, AND BALANCING WORK AND HOME, A PRACTICAL GUIDE TO MANAGING STRESS. Excellent. Both obtainable from Parents at Work (see Useful Addresses).

HEALTHY EATING FOR YOU AND YOUR BABY by Fiona Ford, Robert Fraser and Hilary Dimond (Pan, 1994). This is, as it says, a comprehensive guide to what you should (and shouldn't) eat before, during and after pregnancy. Includes a number of recipes from the original version of my Mother and Baby Book.

GUIDE TO VEGETARIAN LIVING by Peter Cox (Bloomsbury, 1994). Very useful reference book on just about all aspects of vegetarian living with particularly good sections on diet for pregnancy and breastfeeding. Highly recommended.

For more recipes which are quick, cheap, nutritious and enjoyed by children as well as adults, my own books which are particularly relevant are: Oxfam Vegetarian Cookery for Children (Vermilion, 1995), Cheap and Easy (Thorsons, 1995), Vegetarian Fast Food (HarperCollins 1994), The Bean Book (Thorsons, 1994), Rose Elliot's Complete Book of Vegetarian Cookery, HarperCollins 1996.